Conspiracy Theory

A Quincy Harker Demon Hunter Urban Fantasy Novel

(The Skeptoid Guide To The Truth Behind The Theories)

Justin Gray

Published By **Ryan Princeton**

Justin Gray

Conspiracy Theory: A Quincy Harker Demon Hunter Urban Fantasy Novel (The Skeptoid Guide To The Truth Behind The Theories)

ISBN 978-1-77485-619-2

Legal & Disclaimer

The information contained in this ebook is not designed to replace or take the place of any form of medicine or professional medical advice. The information in this ebook has been provided for educational & entertainment purposes only.

The information contained in this book has been compiled from sources deemed reliable, and it is accurate to the best of the Author's knowledge; however, the Author cannot guarantee its accuracy and validity and cannot be held liable for any errors or omissions. Changes are periodically made to this book. You must consult your doctor or get professional medical advice before using any of the suggested remedies, techniques, or information in this book.

Upon using the information contained in this book, you agree to hold harmless the Author from and against any damages, costs, and expenses, including any legal fees potentially resulting from the application of any of the information provided by this guide. This disclaimer applies to any damages or injury caused by the use and application, whether directly or indirectly, of any advice or information presented, whether for breach of contract, tort, negligence, personal injury, criminal intent, or under any other cause of action.

You agree to accept all risks of using the information presented inside this book. You need to consult a professional medical practitioner in order to ensure you are both able and healthy enough to participate in this program.

Table of Contents

Introduction

Conspiracy Theory involves a set of clues that are meant to help narrow down the scope of an investigation. It can also be used to explain an unsolved event or act that is dangerous or illegal. Theorists suggest that many times the person at fault is a group of people or a company.

While this book is meant to entertain you with stories from the best places in the world, it also serves as an informative tool. You'll be able to make your own opinions and weigh down the theories with every page. What's impossible? What's most impossible?

Most of the conspiracies described in this book have already been established. They are enduring theories that require proof. It is up to the reader to determine if these theories sound real or fictitious.

Before you start your journey, please remember that all theories discussed in this book are a mix between fact and fiction. To avoid confusion, each piece of information will be clearly stated in this book.

I am grateful that you downloaded this book. I really hope you enjoy it.

Chapter 1: Area 51

Area 51 is often a part of conspiracy theories. But what did Area 51 do?

What is Area 51, exactly?

Area 51 is also known to be The Ranch, Dreamland, and Groom Lake. The area in Nevada is thought to only be used to test weapons and planes. However, why are so many mystery-seeking UFO enthusiasts eager to uncover the truth?

Let's solve the mystery one by ones:

1. This secretive area was never established. People have been unaware of its existence for decades. Any satellite imagery that is captured can even be deleted. If they can't deleted, then measures will be taken to ensure that they are not visible to the public.

2. Even though the US government repeatedly claimed that Area 51 had never been secret, any research carried out in the area remains highly confidential.

3. Roswell Incident. Area 51 mystery is incomplete without mentioning what occurred in Roswell, New Mexico in 47. A Roswell ranch was the scene of an alleged crash involving an aircraft. Because the area is supposed to be used to test weapons or aircraft, there shouldn't have been any problems with it. So what has sparked the interest of so many?

Mac Brazel mentioned, when he found some parts of an aircraft, that it was hard to 'fathom' what had happened. The military base provided conflicting information on the matter.

4. The last mystery is this: It was not until the 1990s that the U.S. Government issued an official statement. Project Mogul was a top secret project, designed to launch microphones at certain altitudes so that it can detect sound wave. Keep in mind that the Roswell accident occurred in 1947 and Project Mogul only lasted until 1948. This is why they took so long to share the information.

These theories...

1. The debris found wasn't from Project Mogul - it was from an a alien spacecraft. For curiosity sake, some people believed that the alien form of life survived the crash.

2. There have been some reports about the infamous Men in Black. These stories claimed that the Men in Black would visit anyone trying uncover top secrets of the government, and then intimidate them.

3. The government could be collaborating with extraterrestrial life forms for joint ventures, according to other intriguing theories.

4. Area 51 personnel are developing ways to influence the weather. It is possible that they are creating a technology that can teleport people or allow them to perform time travel.

Anatomizing the theories' coffin...

It has been over 6 decades of mystery. Area 51 is a base military, and secretive military bases are common as they often protect national security.

CNN's documentary Area 51: Acknowledged by CNN is the best example of the theories. It features newly released maps and a catchy tagline, which says: Area 51 IS real, but we are sorry, no aliens.

The article stated that the CIA had finally released documents confirming the existence of Area 51. However, not for the purpose that most enthusiasts desire. It only revealed what other writers already reported: Area 51 was a true testing ground for weapons or aircrafts.

Even though this information may not please UFO believers, however briefly, experts state that this is just the beginning. Perhaps there will be more details about the testing ground.

Chapter 2: 9/11 Attacks

One of most tragic and devastating events in history is the 9/11 attack. Many families were left devastated by the tragedy.

Soon after the incident, many conspiracy theories emerged. Some of them are real while others are not.

Here are the most convincing conspiracies regarding the 9/11 attacks.

1. It has to do something with trades

One of 9/11's most compelling conspiracies is that traders are already aware of what will happen, even before the attack.

It was revealed that the stock stocks of American Airlines (United Airlines) were held by a number of put option holders. These airlines were hijacked by the attackers.

A put option is a contract that a trader holds on to a stock. It allows them to sell the stock at the time the stock falls.

It is possible that they don't know the actual bombing. However, it is quite odd that the desire of selling stock in airlines that might be involved with bombing suddenly increased immediately before the incident.

2. Bombs were located in the towers

This theory is plausible. Some survivors claim that the blasts came from the inside of the building as they were trying to escape. This suggests that there were bombs already in place in the tower's various areas before the attack.

Science also showed that even though an aircraft crashed into a building it's fuel would not be able melted the towers' steel frames.

3. How do you explain The Pentagon Attack?

If you take a closer look, the Pentagon attack could be called the strangest event in all of the events surrounding September 11. Reports indicate that the Pentagon building was also attacked on September 11 by suicide bombers aboard the American Airlines plane.

It's odd and funny that the plane created a hole in the ground larger than the plane. Flight 77 (the crash plane) measures 125 ft in width, but the Pentagon impact hole measures only 60 ft.

The most disturbing thing is that the Pentagon side that was allegedly being attacked was unoccupied due to renovations.

Can it be possible there was no actual crash? Could it be that it was an orchestrated missile that destroyed the vacant portion of the building

4. Flight 93 Theories

One of the heroes that emerged from the attack was Flight 93.

According to reports many innocent lives were spared by the passengers who fought hard to stop the plane from colliding into any building.

Flight 93 didn't crash on a particular populated building but crashed in Shanksville.

The most bizarre thing about this story is where the wreckages were found. A large portion of the debris was found to be far from the location of the major crash. Experts suggest that this may have happened if the missile was fired at the plane.

So was Flight 93 deliberately shot at? Some theorists believe so. They believed the passengers discovered the plot to prevent them from surviving. Others claim they were killed in another place after the crash.

5. Hijackers will always be there

After the terrorist attacks of September 11, 2001, the hijackers' names were revealed and, upon further inspection, it was confirmed that they were alive. It's not unusual, as the names of the hijackers were all very common Arabic names (they claimed it was as common than John Smith in USA). However, what is really alarming was that passports of the hijackers survived.

How ironic could it be that the plane crashed that destroyed both towers was able spare the fragile paper documents!

6. Were the calls faked?

One phone call in particular raised suspicion. A male caller contacted his mom and introduced him using his first as well as his last names. What kind of person would do such a thing?

The caller said they were being hijacked and the son simply repeated what he'd already told his mom. That is, "You believe I am right?"

Experts agree that those phone calls were fake.

It is impossible to get cellphone reception above 32000 feet. This is the height that commercial planes are at.

It was even researched, and the success ratio is below 1 percent.

How were they able copy the voice of their callers? Experts believe there is a device capable of recording your voice and quickly morphing another person's voice into yours.

Theorists believe that none of these theories (except for those made by phone calls) have been proven.

Chapter 3: JFK Assassination

John F. Kennedy's beloved president was shot to death in Texas as he walked in an open limousine on November 22, 1963. Many theories circulated about his death. The government did not declare Lee Harvey Oswald the killer. But, they refused to let the theory die.

This section will discuss the compelling theories behind his assassination.

1. Witnesses can die

The possibility that witnesses were intimidated by the Warren Commission or ignored is what made the assassination seem more than just an ordinary murder. A number of witnesses claimed to have smelled gunpowder. However they were not taken seriously by the Warren Commission (commission that was created to investigate JFK assassination).

Some documents were also taken withheld. Witnesses' films were also confiscated.

Worse yet, it was brought into public attention that 103 witnesses were killed inadvertently. Let's also consider Rose Cheramie.

Cheramie was picked by a lieutenant after suffering minor injuries in a vehicle accident. During the drive, she stated that she would visit Texas. When the lieutenant inquired about her plans, she stated that she will go to Texas to pick up some cash, get her baby, kill Kennedy, and then return home.

Surprisingly, the doctor treating her minor injuries said Cheramie also mentioned knowledge of the JKF's killing before the incident. When he told the officer, he just said that he wasn't interested. Cheramie was killed in an accident on September 1965.

Cheramie used heroin and was reported to have mentioned to her doctor during her stay in the hospital that she worked as a nurse for Jack Ruby. Ruby is the one who killed Oswald.

2. Mafia Work

Before the incident, President JFK sent Carlos Marcello (a mobster leader) to deportation.

This was after his brother was accused of creating crimes while serving as a US attorney. Marcelo threatened JFK once he had found his way to the US.

Some reports suggest that he confessed his crime while he was still in prison.

This story was believed to be true by many theorists, especially since Jack Ruby was also associated with the mobster.

3. Connection to the government

A majority of people also believed that the government was involved, especially the vice-president during Kennedy's reign-- Lyndon Johnson. They suggested that Johnson was motivated enough. He wanted to become president, and he hated Kennedy. He was afraid that Kennedy would drop him from the election ticket.

Some believe he was helped along by wealthy people, who thought that they would reap the benefits of his presidency. Bush is believed to have assisted him in the crime.

Johnson himself created the Warren Commission which, according legends, intimidated and ignored witnesses.

3. It's CIA

If a murder occurs, the Central Intelligence Agency may be identified as the suspect. The JFK assassination does not fall within this category.

It was a well-known reality that The Bay of Pigs Invasion was unsuccessful. People believe that after this failure, a rift between the CIA & president formed. This gap forced CIA to retaliate against him by assassinating his body.

This theory was made plausible when it was discovered that the CIA actually had planned some assassinations. An unsuccessful plot was launched against Ngo Dinh Diem in Vietnam, and a successful plot was mounted against Fidel Castro in Cuba.

4. Fidel Castro had to be the one to do it.

Castro may have wanted to retaliate for the fact Castro was killed by the CIA. Lyndon Johnson even believed it. Castro's reasoning is still plausible.

At the time, an attack on Cuba would have appeared too obvious (given their relationship is so fragile), and too dangerous. Consider how capable the US would appear if they were to seek retaliation.

Others claimed Castro was Castro's enemy in the hopes that the US would assassinate him.

5. The president's closest friends did it

As unbelievable as it may sound, some speculated that those present during the assassination were the ones responsible.

Jackie Kennedy is Jackie's husband. Jackie was holding a bouquet filled with flowers. People said she could shoot a gun from a handgun without anyone knowing. It was even said that she was an undercover criminal.

Second was the driver, who is believed to have been assisted from the man in the passenger's seat.

Kennedy's security detail was last but not least. This accusation began after an expert suggested the firing was accidental. A book titled Mortal Error published it. It was later proven false, and the accused guard even brought charges against the authors.

These theories seem compelling but the truth is that they are not based on solid evidence. It is important to remember that there was a large crowd at Kennedy's assassination. This would have been the time when anyone near him pulled out a gun and shot Kennedy in the head.

6. Signal from Umbrellaman

Footage showed that during the assassination, a man was opening and shutting his umbrella while the president's limousine passed. It's suspicious that he was carrying an umbrella even though it wasn't raining. Theorists think it might have been a signal from the gunman.

7. The Babushka Lady

Footage showed that, except for the Umbrella Man (pictured), a Babushka Lady with a camera held to her face never left a scene, even when people looked for cover.

The FBI later asked Babushka's lady to make a statement. Beverly Oliver, an elderly woman, was there and said that people had asked her for the film from her camera. But they never returned it.

Babushka in Russian means grandmother. Her outfit was typical of a Russian grandmother's, consisting of a coat and head scarf. Additionally, she was wearing sunglasses that made her face more visible. This led to some people speculating that she was actually a man disguised.

Chapter 4: Conspiracy Theories Concerning UFOs & Aliens

Many conspiracy theories are being circulated about UFOs and aliens. This section will cover the most popular, and thus most trusted theories about extraterrestrials.

1. The Majestic 12

The Majestic 12 - also called MJ 12 - is a group that is responsible for investigating extraterrestrial artifacts. It includes scientists, politicians and military personnel. The MJ 12 was formed, it is believed, by Harry Truman in 1947.

The UFOlogists circulated certain documents and the Revelation to the Majestic 12 was born. These documents were actually sent in the format of film. Film developed from these images contained photos of printed documents.

Some briefing was given for Operation Majestic 12 in the documents. They described how Roswell was covered up and how the spacecraft would be examined in order to discover extraterrestrial technology that could be used in the future. They should also be open to the possibility of interacting with other life forms.

However, the government confirmed that these documents were fakes and did not have any connection to them.

2. Project Blue Book

Project Blue Book is very transparent. The government announced that Project Blue Book had two main purposes: the first was to identify aliens capable of threatening our national security and the second was to further analyze UFO data.

Project Blue Book was, according to some theories, a coverup to distract people's attention off the Majestic12. They claimed that, although the project lasted many years, the time spent on the studies was minimal.

Project Blue Book eventually revealed these two pieces.

1. There was no evidence of UFO or Alien activity which could threaten security.

2. Although they received more than 12000 UFO reporting reports, further investigation revealed that many of them were misidentifications.

3. Ancient Astronauts

One of the most intriguing and plausible theories ever is that of the ancient astronauts. This theory suggests that aliens have already visited earth and made contact primitive humans before we even had the simplest technologies.

Some believe that extraterrestrials are responsible for building some of the most extraordinary structures in the universe, like Stonehenge and Pyramids.

This theory is even more amazing because it suggests that those alien beings were deities from the ancient past. They stated that they believed the primitive minds of our forefathers mistook them to be divinities because of their advanced technology.

4. The New World Order

The New World Order or NWO is one the most popular UFO and alien theories. According to this theory, aliens are always with us. Not just for a few more years, but thousands of years.

Theorists believe that aliens are capable to shape-shift into realistic human forms. They can also live among us in freedom, and without detection due to the fact that they are being protected by the government.

This is the main purpose for this cover up. That's right, to seize control of our precious earth!

Chapter 5: Ten of the most compelling conspiracies around the world

Instead of focusing on extraterrestrial beings let us focus on some of these infamous conspiracies. These are the ones that many people find fascinating and believable. These theories cover everything from cover ups to corruption of government officials.

Some of these theories even survived decades. It seems that clarity is still elusive.

1. Turkey: Corruption

There was an anti-corruption campaign in Turkey that took place just recently. It saw more than 50 arrests. There was reportedly an overflow of evidence. Many of those arrested have a close connection to Recep TAYYIP Erdogan, the current Prime Minister.

Some theorists argue that there was never any corruption and that if it did, it was much smaller than it appeared back then.

Evidently, Turkey's economy thrived during Erdogan's reign.

2. AIDS is a premeditated criminal offense

Some theorists believed the fatal AIDS, which gradually kills its victim, was a premeditated criminal act committed by the US government (especially the CIA) to wipe out gay men. Speculators aren't convinced that the virus originated out of Africa. Instead, they believe that it was created in one US military laboratory.

The process is like this: CIA agents injected HIV-infected men from Africa using the Hepatitis Vaccine that had been in the testing stage.

The same applies to other diseases. Some people believe they were deliberately designed so that vaccines are possible and people are scared enough that they will buy them.

But is it possible for this conspiracy theory to be true? Many believe that this conspiracy theory is true. Let's start by looking at how various health agencies explain the pronounced origins and spread of AIDS. According to the explanation, AIDS is most likely a virus that originated in a monkey. As Africans prepared the infected Chimpanzee, some might have received a splash blood. That blood would have entered their open wounds and eventually caused the infection.

But, many articles have disputed this "explanation". Origin Of Aids actually says this is impossible. Let's learn more:

The Royal Society of London had a conference in 2005. The objective was to debate, brainstorm, solve, and ultimately eradicate HIV/AIDS. Many world-renowned scientists collaborated to come up with the idea that HIV could be derived from a contaminated vaccination, which was then given to many African villager.

Their theories were focused on OPV. Oral Polio Vaccine. These cells were confirmed to have been contaminated with at most two cancer cells. Thus, it was likely that it would contain other viruses such as HIV-1. This virus is the most severe and widely spread to date.

After many arguments, discussions and debates, scientists and researchers realized that although this idea was possible they could not prove it to have been true.

They were forced to change to a possible alternative. Dr. Gerald Myers (from Los Alamos Laboratory near New Mexico) and Chief Sequence Analyst for the US Government presented to his colleagues the notion that zoonosis - or cross-contamination from animals with humans - couldn't have occurred.

He argued, "AIDS started in the mid-70s and lab tests showed there were at minimum 10 subtypes in Africa." If HIV only came from a small amount of blood from a chimpanzee, how can there be ten? Dr. Myers suggested that it must have been iatrogenic.

Myers concluded that it wasn't farfetched to think that 10 or so subtypes could have come from a single animal. Or perhaps a group of animals. But he stated that "the vaccine hypothesis opens the door to a more punctuated AIDS source."

So far, we have two theories: First, monkeys are not used in the manufacturing of OPVs. Second,

AIDS might have been an iatrogenic disorder. The only possible explanation for HIV/AIDS is if other contaminated vaccines were administered to the African villagers. The clues to this are obvious: The vaccine should have included some chimpanzees cells and should not have been given at the time that AIDS began (around mid-1970s).

Hepatitis vaccine B is the closest answer.

His award-winning book Emerging Viruses AIDS & EBOLA: Nature, Accident, or Intentional, was published. Harvard graduate Dr. Leonard Horowitz presented some compelling evidences that the National Institute of Health used Chimpanzees, which can be contaminated with many viruses, to produce hundreds of HepatitisB vaccines. They were distributed to Central Africa alongside homosexual men from New York City.

It's not surprising, is it? It is shocking to discover that intelligent and powerful people can manipulate someone's health. They can kill thousands or hundreds of people using a single syringe. And they promise the vaccine will protect them against any kind of illness.

Although we don't know for certain, it is plausible.

3. Paul McCartney actually died

Let's not forget the infamous "Paul is Dead" theory. The story suggested McCartney, the man behind the very popular 'The Beatles,' actually died in an accident that took place in 1967. After the incident, students at one Campus University highlighted the clues. This, of course, ignited the interest of many.

One clue was provided by the Abbey Road album's cover. The band seems to be crossing a pedestrian lane. The cover appears to have been part of a funeral procession. Starr was dressed as the mourner, Harrison was dressed as the digger and McCartney is the only person without shoes (the deceased person to be interred).

These accounts can be used to conceal the messages of the artist's album.

According to speculation, The Beatles may have hired someone who looked similar to him in order to pose as an impostor. However, if true then the impostor still exists. Would you like to know more about evidence that Paul McCartney was dead? Here are their names:

1) On the cover for their album Sgt Pepper's Lonely Hearts Band you will see a yellow wreath in the bottom right. The wreath looked like a basse guitar and many believe it was the Beatle's way of honoring Paul who, by then, had been replaced with an impostor.

But, the truth of it is, Beatles fans claimed that it was not Paul who did it, but Stu Sutcliffe, their friend and former member. He died in 1962. John chose Stu, the original bass player, when all Beatles members were allowed to choose from a list of famous personalities to appear in the cover.

2) John Lennon said something in Strawberry Fields Forever's opening.

Fans who were firm in their support for the band supported Lennon. They argued that

Lennon said these words to defame the theorists, as the group was aware of the death rumor at the time.

Paul (or his impostor?) would later claim that Lennon was not the one who buried Paul. Lennon's words "I buried Paul" were not what he meant, but he did say "cranberry Sauce". Others suggested that he could simply have said: "I buried Paol", rather than saying: "cranberry Sauce." Whatever the case, this recording was still able t fuel the minds many mystery fanatics.

3) Then came the notorious Billy Shears. You can hear the Sgt. Pepper's Band, it is possible to hear them introduce a man called "Billy Shears". Since then, many people have assumed this Billy had replaced Paul McCartney.

It was not as simple as that. GringoStarr sang the next verse when this Billy was introduced. The band said they were being put under a lot pressure during this time. They ended up with seven best-selling albums. But they didn't know what to do next. So, to ease tension, the band decided to take on another personality. Billy Shears was apparently the result.

4) Lastly you will hear statements like "Paul died" in the back masking of certain songs such as I'm So Tired, A Day in the Life. I miss Paul, and I miss him," as well as "Will Paul Be There As Superman?"

Experts dispute the claims of back masking, however intriguing they may be. They claim that anyone could hear whatever they wanted to hear, provided they can concentrate.

Paul is, as the rest of the world knows, still very much alive today. Or is it an impostor of Paul?

4. Electronic Banking

Many believe that ATM card use (both debit as credit) is a scheme to completely eliminate money bills. If people are already dependent on paperless purchase, then the 'higher' ups (whoever they happen to be) will create a massive glitch in electronic banking that will destroy the system.

The result of this theoretical process? Slavery is being brought back into practice.

5. The Bermuda Triangle Mystery

Bermuda has been taking people out of their homes for a while so it's not surprising that it would be included in one of the most popular conspiracy theories.

It is true that several vessels were reported to have vanished upon travel to the Devil's triangle. Additionally, it was stated that a compass glitch can also occur (theorists state that if you're in Bemuda, your GPS will point you to Northern instead of the magnetic North, which is what is normal).

Experts agree that Bermuda's number of lost ships and planes is similar to other areas. It's because Bermuda is so well-traveled.

6. Death of Princess Diana

What can we forget the terrible accident that claimed Diana's life? People have come to value her kind nature since she was married, to Prince Charles.

Unfortunately, her marriage was not to last and she separated from the prince in 1996. 2 years after their divorce, she was involved in an accident that led to her death.

Theorists believe it to be the Royal Family. They believe that Dodi Alayed, her boyfriend at the time, didn't want Princess Diana to marry Dodi. The possibility that she knew some dark secret about her royal family led to speculations that she was attempting to kill herself.

Another theory says that the paparazzi had been following their car at extremely high speed, and this caused the collision.

7. The Tuskegee Syphilis study

This is perhaps the saddest and most tragic cover-ups in the history of both politics and health care. 600 men were examined by the Tuskegee Public Health Service. Almost half of them were already infected. The problem? The problem was that half of the participants didn’t receive any treatment, despite having been told so.

Syphilis, if untreated, can cause chronic and severe injuries to the individual's internal organs. It may even lead to death. The good news about Syphilis is that a simple penicillin was available back in 1947.

Bad news! The bad news is that they didn't get the cure from the health care staff, even though the study was done between 1932 and 1972. They could have easily given penicillin directly to the patients starting in 1947. But they chose not. They wanted to see if syphilis would improve without medication. So they used trickery to get the information they needed.

They also wanted information about the effects on the disease. The PHS actually let 128 people perish. 28 died of syphilis and 100 died of related diseases. It was discovered that the STD was contracted also by 20 wives and 19 children.

Five main reasons the Tuskegee trial was illegal and unethical are listed below:

1. There was not informed consent. Informed consent means asking for permission after the patient/participant has been made fully aware of all details about the experiment. This information should be provided in a way that he can fully comprehend the entire process, including risks and advantages.

People in the Tuskegee Experiment were misinformed. They didn't know they would be in a research programme. They believed that they were being provided the cure. They did not know that spinal tap is still dangerous and was considered dangerous by the medical community.

This meant that the participants were left with no choice. They thought they would get all of the good things and none if the bad. So why would they need to decline the offer? Many of them wouldn't have turned down the offer if professionals had spoken truthfully to them.

2. PHS "forced" their participants to sign an agreement for the health department's autopsy to be conducted on their bodies. To make matters worse, they added that if participants

signed the agreement, their funeral costs will be covered.

The lure of death insurance and cure was attractive for participants, who were, in the end, illiterate, impoverished black men. It was as if PHS held the men in their hands.

3. Cure was denied, even though it could be obtained. This was a clear statement that PHS was not pro-life.

4. The health department used misleading advertisements. The slogans included: Last Chance for Special Therapy Free of Charge. Even though there was no treatment available, they designed the slogan to make it so people would not resist the offer.

5. It was discrimination. PHS believed that the study could benefit humanity, but they neglected to consider the welfare of the participants' families. It was as if the "humankind" didn't exist. Perhaps it was because they were of African descent.

Chapter 6: Fake Moon Landing

After almost 40 years, many still believe that Armstrong's moon-landing was a hoax. According to speculators the US government used to be so determined to beat Russia in space exploration that it tried to shoot the moon landing.

Stanley Kubrick is believed to have directed the film. A space movie in 1968 with an almost identical setting was used in Kubrick's movie A Space Odyssey. Two theories are possible for this "filming suspicion: the first is that Kubrick was approached by the US Government in 1968 to see how real his film was. The second theory is that Kubrick was "groomed" to perform the task of faking exploration and that the movie was simply a "practice."

Kubrick's film The Shining gave clues to enthusiasts who are looking for subtle signs. In one scene, the child was wearing an Apollo 11-t-shirt. This was for enthusiasts to indicate that Kubrick was involved in the mission.

The second clue was a line found at Jack Nicholson's typing desk. It read: "All play and no work makes Jack boring." This is a statement that many people are not aware of.

The waving flag added fuel to that fire. Because there should not be wind in the vacuum space, it sparked into an uncontrollable wildfire. What's the secret to that flag waving? NASA said NASA was correct in defending NASA, claiming that the flag is moving due to the force of burying it.

Even some scientists believe the three astronauts who died at the equipment test for the first space mission were executed because of their plans to expose the truth. You can find more evidence here.

1) There was no crater visible on the surface of the planet after the spacecraft landed. Enthusiasts argue that at the very least, the spacecraft should've left a "blast" crater. NASA photographs show that the surface underneath the module appears unaffected. This is because it seems like the craft was placed there naturally. NASA, however, claimed that there is no gravity on the Moon and therefore the

impact was not as difficult as when it would land on earth.

2) The shadows. The sun is the only light source that shines brightly on the moon. This is something everyone is aware of. This made it logical to assume all the shadows would run parallel. However, it wasn't.

Some photographs taken by the administration show shadows that are spread out in various directions. This suggests that there were many light sources. Many claim this is evidence that the moon landing took places on film sets where lights could be used.

NASA didn't have their own light source. That would be a lie, even though a believer would love it. The moon's uneven terrain was the reason they were presented with this theory. However, when presented with this theory, they were unable to stop blaming the moon's uneven terrain.

3) Astronauts shouldn't have died. Many people who are experts in space exploration believe that astronauts should be cooked during their journey to the moon. Before they can reach their destination, they will have to go through the Van Allen Radiation Belt - a radiation-packed swathe held in position by gravity.

NASA had repeatedly maintained that the astronauts didn't remain on the belt for very long, even though they did traverse it. The craft moved at such a fast speed that it was possible for the astronauts to get very little radiation. In addition, the spacemen claimed that the module's inside and outside were covered with layers upon layer of aluminum.

4) The hanging thing. Close-up of one of the Apollo 12 Mission astronauts. The object was

clearly visible in the spaceman's helmet. It looked hanging, but it wasn't clear what it was. Others assumed it was a lighting source, but no one knows for sure. NASA is not even close to the matter.

5) The lack of stars was perhaps the most convincing argument against the authenticity. NASA took photos of all the lunar landings and not one photo showed a shining Star -- there was no space between the Earth and the Moon.

https://en.wikipedia.org/wiki/Apollo_11#/media/File:Apollo_11_lunar_module.jpg

https://en.wikipedia.org/wiki/Apollo_11#/media/File:Apollo_11_Earth.jpg

NASA did not handle this theory well. Most people think they gave an "excuse". When asked why there was no piece of star in the space, they replied that it was because of the quality and lack of stars. To put it another way, speculators laughed at them. Although there were many good photos out there, it still didn't contain any of the many constellations. You can also capture stars with photos from Earth. How could that be?

Believers in the fake moon landing claim that NASA deliberately left them out as they couldn’t determine how to map stars in the setting. Stars are in a given position. People could not determine if their position was wrong.

6) The rock with the letter C in it. Believe it, but a featured rock from the moon was found with a perfect letter "C". It wasn't accidental, the way it was "written", was so perfect. NASA offered contradicting statements about it. First they said that it was most likely a mistake from the photo developer. Second, they said that he intended to include it as a joke. Finally, they suggested that it could have been a hair strand which was accidentally included during the development of the image.

7) Background edit. NASA released two photographs and stated that they were taken miles apart. NASA claimed one photo included the space module and the other none. The problem? It was evident that the background

was the exact same when one of the images was compared to the other. From the curves and cast shadows, it was identical. Theorists believe that it was because they merely altered the photos in an effort to share as many photos as possible.

NASA was quick to defend their position, saying that the moon was only smaller, and therefore it was easier for us to see things in a more detailed perspective.

You can't help but have doubts based on all these clues. But, let's not forget that the astronauts landing on the moon brought back hundreds if rock samples which were confirmed. Or they weren't?

Chapter 7: Reptiles Head Us

If it isn't aliens leading us then they could be reptiles. Reptilian Leaders, similar to New World Order theory, suggests shape-shifting reptiles are in our midst. They are well-known for being very influential, as is Queen Elizabeth.

David Icke was a BBC journalist who also promoted this theory. Icke has even published several books. His books mentioned that these reptile leaders could be the people behind powerful organizations such a Illuminati or Freemasons.

David Icke achieved the title of Paranoid in the Decade for his efforts in the 1990s. But was it really true or was he paranoid?

David Icke is who?

David Icke was a Leicesterian, England-born man who lived a simple life. His childhood was filled playing football. It's no surprise that he decided to make a career out sports as an adult. Unfortunately, he developed knee arthritis that eventually spread to his whole body.

He quickly realized football was out of the question and switched his focus to sports broadcasting. Soon, he was delivering the news on athletics for BBC radio and television.

In his 80s, he started looking into other treatments to relieve his chronic arthritis. David began to notice politics and the Green Party around this same time. After being fired at BBC over tax problems, he refocused his energies on being an influential leader of Greens.

David found that things were getting more interesting.

David said that during those trying times, David was awakened. A "presence", or something like that, was present around him and was trying transmit some type of message. He believed that his desire to understand these messages led him on a spiritual path. It eventually taught him many conspiracy theories that were not familiar. After a spiritual visit to Peru, he left politics for an unknown reason.

Loosened, Screws

David Icke did the Unthinkable in 1991.

He was laughed at by many, though they were not open to the idea. He mentioned how walking down the streets was an easy task in those days. Everybody thought David was crazy. David experienced a sense of freedom after all the ridicule. In one interview, he said that after receiving the worst mockery from his family, he lost interest in it all until it was irrelevant what other people thought of him.

For the next decade, he was relentless in his research and travels. He also gave long talks to people about who is really the ruler of the world.

Reptilian Hybrids are the Rule of the World

David's idea, to be fair, was not original. In fact it was already mentioned decades ago. Many mystery enthusiasts believed that aliens are already in our world and were being watched by us. They wanted power, enough to be able to take over the government and turn us into their slaves.

David's theory wasn't much more advanced.

According to him, the world's rulers have been divided into some type of class. This gives the impression that they are divided by their race, country, religion, preferences and careers. But in fact, all these leaders belong to one team, specifically one family line.

David asked David to prove that he was right. They all had one common lineage: from Bush to Clinton and the current leader Barrack Obama. Perhaps the public doesn't care about voting at all. Yes, it was a contest, but the winner wasn’t the one who received the most votes. The winner would be the one with more royal genes.

David stated that even outside the realm of politics, the highly intact bloodline could also be found among other powerful people. These powerful people include bankers and pharmaceutical company owners as well as food industry tycoons.

For instance, Madonna, Brad Pitt (Mrs. Monroe), Brad Pitt (Brad Pitt) and Tom Hanks are all of royal descent. Coincidence? David thinks otherwise.

He indicates that power and money are two of the main factors in our world. Money comes from businesses and banks. Power is the result of fame and leadership. That's why they don't just focus on politics or government. They knew that it would be more difficult to conquer all of humanity. David responded to a question regarding how this "secret ruling", saying that these reptilian leaders were able manipulate DNA and people.

When did this happen, David? It must have been a long while ago. David claims that at one time, reptilians entered our world, and they began "interbreeding", possibly not physically, but through manipulation. David claimed that the brains of people are "fundamental" reptilian genetics.

Over the long-term, hybrids developed from this interbreeding. They were able to understand more than people. They had more advantage and were therefore more useful. These hybrids spread across the globe, knowing full well that they are superior to everyone else.

They would become the Royal family, leaders of dynasties and powerful businessmen. David believes that it was because of this that royalties are often reluctant to share their wealth, so that the family's genes won't be lost.

Behind Closed Doors

David spoke openly about the annual close doors meetings of global leaders. He explained that instead of discussing economy, terrorists, or climate, the rulers practice rituals that most people would consider satanism. David also said that the rulers are bound to a religion that was established at the very beginning of human civilization.

There are many rituals performed behind closed door doors, including blood sacrifices, sexual activities and chanting. John F. Kennedy would be a good example. President Kennedy, apparently, attempted to make public the activities of the secret society in one his famous speeches. The following are just a portion of the exact quotes.

"The very term "secrecy", while it is offensive in a free society, is also a problem in our history. Secret societies, secret oaths, secret proceedings and secret societies are all things we reject as human beings. Our opposition is based on a single-minded and ruthless conspiracy ..."that relies only on covert methods to expand its influence

David also disclosed that the Catholic Catholic Church had played a major role in this expanding influence. He then pointed out Pope Benedict XVI's resignation to make it even more convincing. David claimed the pope was blackmailed because he had released information to Vatican about the Catholic Church's homosexual activities and child abuse. Were there any supporting evidence for this claim. Evidently.

Neil Brick, a victim in this abuse, also founded SMART Organization, which was established in 1995. SMART stands as Stop Mind Control & Ritual Abuse Today. Neil stated that each year thousands are brought into the Vatican to have their minds manipulated for sexual activities.

Worse yet, these secret meetings occur in different locations around the globe. This is evident in the bizarre gathering that took place at Bohemian Grove California. There, about 2000 members from the elite gathered to celebrate the "Summer Festival". In reality, however, they were performing inexplicable actions. Alex Jones was able to access the secret meeting and it can be viewed on YouTube.

Which do you think about this? While it may seem counterintuitive to consider Grasping David's theories as a priority, it is something we should all acknowledge.

Chapter 8: The Subliminal Effect of Subliminal Signals

Experts claim that marketers use subliminal messages to manipulate our subconscious minds and make us more likely to purchase their products or use their services. Subliminal messages within advertisements may not reach our conscious, but they trigger something that causes our subconscious to be more open to the idea.

Advertise another product (something people will enjoy) in a low-profile way. The product will be bought by the people because they liked it. The most used subliminal message is'sex. Why? Because sex appeals strongly to people.

What exactly is subliminal messaging?

Subliminal messages are actually quite simple. If you don't notice an advertisement for an item, you will not be as interested in it. Experts explained that our conscious brain doesn't recognize subliminal messages, but it can be seen by the more powerful subconscious. These messages are best inserted via audio or visually.

It is possible to not see a product being displayed in public, but it may be there. Advertisers and promoters add appealing words, phrases or pictures in between the movie frames at a speed that is so fast you might not even be able read them or notice them. Make no mistake, the subconscious part of your mind saw it.

James Vicary, who is considered the founder of subliminal ads, claimed that his movie had given him subliminal clues which enabled him to convince people to buy Coca-Cola and popcorn. James Vicary allegedly added phrases like "Drink Coca-Cola," and "Hungry?" to the movie. Popcorn !"-- Both products saw a huge increase in sales after the movie.

This "effect" was a source of mass panic when people heard about it. As you would expect, people didn't like being told what the right thing to do. Thus, the idea of being controlled without them knowing was horrendous. These people believed that the subliminal clues (whatever they were) could be used in order to obtain political power. This is how conspiracy theories about it emerged.

The only problem? James Vicary lied. He didn’t perform the experiment. Instead, he simply told a scientific fraud. Do you think that this means that mental conditioning by subliminal clues was not possible?

It doesn't.

Subliminal Messages Can Be Real

Although James Vicary claimed that his experiment was a hoax a Harvard 1999 study found that subliminal messaging may actually be true. They asked people to enter a space and play computer-based games.

Unbeknownst of them, the games were incorporated along with a group word: one set had positive terms like "accomplished," 'astute' and 'wise", and the other set had words like dependent>, senile> and diseased>.

These words were shown in a very short time -- about one thousandthth of a second. Therefore, it was impossible for participants not to have read them. Surprisingly those gamers who were shown the positive words left much quicker than those who were exposed to the negative words.

Why are people afraid of subliminal message?

People are not afraid of the messages. In truth, they are worried about the possibility of being tricked into believing, feeling, or buying certain things. Because messages are subtle, they can be placed in any song, movie, or photo. Let's take Disney movies and animation films as an example.

Disney films are a delight for both children and adults. They offer colorful stories that teach moral lessons as well as entertaining entertainment. It's easy enough to assume that people all over the globe would welcome a Disney film. But, what if you are sending subtle messages to your children, and yourself, that could alter their and your perceptions of the world?

Simba, a main character in The Lion King, collapses at the top. The dust flies to the sky and forms the word "Sex" discretely. Aladdin can be heard saying "Come, good kitty... take of and go ..."-- nothing wrong with this statement. But, when critics analyzed the episode they discovered that Aladdin was really saying "Good teenagers. Take your clothes off."

Needless not, many parents were horrified. Another example was in "The Rescuers", which featured a poster of an unclothed woman in one of its scenes. Although it was blurred slightly, the poster was clearly identifiable. The film was also shown very quickly but critics were still capable of catching it.

This film was first released in 1977. Disney recalled at minimum 4 million copies due to outrage. When the film was remade, Disney insisted that the poster had been removed. The question here is why the poster was included when they knew that it should be suitable for children and families.

Disney was also accused by sending discriminatory messages in addition to the subliminal clues relating to sexuality. One of the most famous is the scene in The Little Mermaid that saw Sebastian, a Jamaican speaker crab, singing Under the Sea. These lyrics say it all:

"Up on shore, they work all the day

They slave away out in the sun

While we devotin'

Full time floatin’

Under the water ..."

Parents suggested Disney was trying too much to influence their children's thinking by suggesting that living a nonworking lifestyle and others slaving off is the definition if a happy life.

Dumbo, in addition to The Little Mermaid's story, was also traced by some sort of discriminatory message. In one scene, black men and animals worked at circus while singing the following song: "We Work All Day, We Work All Night, We Never Learned to Read and Write, We Work All Night, We Work All Day, and Can't Wait to Spend Our Pay Off."

Worse yet, if we look at the workers closely, we see that their faces were missing. As if to suggest that they are not important enough and should not have distinguishing features.

The answer to the obvious question: Why are people afraid about subliminal message? Imagine millions and millions of children being introduced to the idea of sexuality and discrimination without their parents ever knowing. This is scary.

Why are subliminal signals inserted?

Although this is a difficult question to answer, most believers believe that subliminal messages are used as a way to control the universe. Disney is one example. They are accused of "preparing" the youth for the New World Order.

Worse yet, many people pointed that Walt Disney was a member of the notorious Illuminati. Just by looking at their logo, you'll see that "Walt Disney", which had three 6-like figures, is almost straight. In most cultures, the symbol of evil is 6-6-6. Mickey Mouse is also often seen with a witch's head covered in glitter, as though he is casting a spell.

Disney is not the only company using subliminal message. There are thousands more.

Chapter 9: Holocaust Never Happened

https://en.wikipedia.org/wiki/The_Holocaust#/media/File:Selection_Birkenau_ramp.jpg

https://en.wikipedia.org/wiki/The_Holocaust#/media/File:Nazi_Holocaust_by_bullets_-_Jewish_mass_grave_near_Zolochiv,_west_Ukraine.jpg

Despite the worldwide outrage, tension, and noise it created, the Holocaust didn't actually happen. That's at least the view of those who believe that the Holocaust is a hoax. This theory has been called "The Holocaust Denial".

What is Holocaust Denial, and how can it be explained?

Holocaust Denialism claims there was never a Holocaust. The majority of Jews who died in WWII were not killed by torture, gas chambers or forced labor. The rest of the Jews who managed to survive were relocated.

This idea isn't all that popular in the United States. In fact, only 2% disbelieved what happened in Auschwitz camps. However, 28% believe the Holocaust Denial is true. The widespread denial led many European countries

to order that any attempt to deny the Holocaust be punished with law. Did you realize that a British bishop was excommunicated for his beliefs as Holocaust deniers?

This idea wasn't something that was just thrown out to get attention. It was a result of some solid arguments. David Irving, an eminent historian, also denied the Holocaust. He even created a 2-hour documentary on it.

One of his arguments were the gas chambers. These gas chambers were known to be used to poison Jewish prisoners with cyanide (or another poisonous gas). David claimed the chambers were intended for the prisoner's clothing, and not for their own use.

Some people call them revisionists.

Hutton Gibson is the father of Mel Gibson. How is it possible that they were open to this idea and not genocide? Revisionists said it was because there was no document about the genocide that was signed. However, there was a pending agreement showing that the

https://en.wikipedia.org/wiki/The_Holocaust#/media/File:Selection_Birkenau_ramp.jpg

https://en.wikipedia.org/wiki/The_Holocaust#/media/File:Nazi_Holocaust_by_bullets_-_Jewish_mass_grave_near_Zolochiv,_west_Ukraine.jpg

Despite the worldwide outrage, tension, and noise it created, the Holocaust didn't actually happen. That's at least the view of those who believe that the Holocaust is a hoax. This theory has been called "The Holocaust Denial".

What is Holocaust Denial, and how can it be explained?

Holocaust Denialism claims there was never a Holocaust. The majority of Jews who died in WWII were not killed by torture, gas chambers or forced labor. The rest of the Jews who managed to survive were relocated.

This idea isn't all that popular in the United States. In fact, only 2% disbelieved what happened in Auschwitz camps. However, 28% believe the Holocaust Denial is true. The widespread denial led many European countries

to order that any attempt to deny the Holocaust be punished with law. Did you realize that a British bishop was excommunicated for his beliefs as Holocaust deniers?

This idea wasn't something that was just thrown out to get attention. It was a result of some solid arguments. David Irving, an eminent historian, also denied the Holocaust. He even created a 2-hour documentary on it.

One of his arguments were the gas chambers. These gas chambers were known to be used to poison Jewish prisoners with cyanide (or another poisonous gas). David claimed the chambers were intended for the prisoner's clothing, and not for their own use.

Some people call them revisionists.

Hutton Gibson is the father of Mel Gibson. How is it possible that they were open to this idea and not genocide? Revisionists said it was because there was no document about the genocide that was signed. However, there was a pending agreement showing that the

https://en.wikipedia.org/wiki/The_Holocaust#/media/File:Selection_Birkenau_ramp.jpg

https://en.wikipedia.org/wiki/The_Holocaust#/media/File:Nazi_Holocaust_by_bullets_-_Jewish_mass_grave_near_Zolochiv,_west_Ukraine.jpg

Despite the worldwide outrage, tension, and noise it created, the Holocaust didn't actually happen. That's at least the view of those who believe that the Holocaust is a hoax. This theory has been called "The Holocaust Denial".

What is Holocaust Denial, and how can it be explained?

Holocaust Denialism claims there was never a Holocaust. The majority of Jews who died in WWII were not killed by torture, gas chambers or forced labor. The rest of the Jews who managed to survive were relocated.

This idea isn't all that popular in the United States. In fact, only 2% disbelieved what happened in Auschwitz camps. However, 28% believe the Holocaust Denial is true. The widespread denial led many European countries

to order that any attempt to deny the Holocaust be punished with law. Did you realize that a British bishop was excommunicated for his beliefs as Holocaust deniers?

This idea wasn't something that was just thrown out to get attention. It was a result of some solid arguments. David Irving, an eminent historian, also denied the Holocaust. He even created a 2-hour documentary on it.

One of his arguments were the gas chambers. These gas chambers were known to be used to poison Jewish prisoners with cyanide (or another poisonous gas). David claimed the chambers were intended for the prisoner's clothing, and not for their own use.

Some people call them revisionists.

Hutton Gibson is the father of Mel Gibson. How is it possible that they were open to this idea and not genocide? Revisionists said it was because there was no document about the genocide that was signed. However, there was a pending agreement showing that the

Germans had considered using Madagascar to relocate many Jewish families.

We have the proof

But does that mean the multitude of evidence supporting the Holocaust's existence is invalidated by the lack or documentation? However, revisionists believe it does. Below is "proof" that many concentration camps were not exterminated.

1) Eli Wiesel's novel "Night" recounts the events in Auschwitz during WWII. Not one mention is made about gas chambers. While the book only consists of a little over 100 pages, something as grave as gas poisoning ought to have been mentioned if it was widespread in concentration camps. Eli was presented with the option of either withdrawing with the Germans or remaining under the Soviet Union's protection at the conclusion of the book.

2) The Holocaust claimed to be responsible for millions of deaths; if that were true, then there would be tons upon lots of bodies and skeletons. But nobody found anything. While

there were still bodies around, they weren't 6 million. Believers claimed the Nazis burned the bodies in an attempt to cover up the massacre. But, if so, the ashes should be thick. Again, none.

What's more? The Auschwitz camps, which were only accessible to Soviet Poland up until the 1950s after the rescue, did not become available to Jews until that time. So it was very possible that "evidence" had been altered or worse planted.

3) US intelligence was present in Auschwitz at the peak of the Auschwitz murders. Because Auschwitz was where synthetic rubbers could be made, this was why the US intelligence in the area was so important. If gassing had been occurring in the camp why didn't US intelligence inform it?

4) Post WWII books by famous wartime leaders didn’t mention genocide. Churchill and Eisenhower were some of these leaders. How come they didn't relate the story? Unless, ofcourse, gas poisoning never happened.

5) Holocaust claimed 6,000,000 Jews. But, according to statistics, that number must be at least 13. Although females can give rise to multiple children at once, the Jewish community did not perform a census that would have reported this kind of fertility.
6) Perhaps the best argument offered by the believers is that even the Germans confessed to the genocide. Revisionists, however, have clarified that these admissions were made using torture. The German soldiers in the Nuremberg Trial were held captive for several hours by their (mostly Jewish interrogators).

7) Finally, the greatest enemy of deniers comes when believers ask: "Why do people lie about Holocaust?" While a normal person wouldn't be able understand why someone, or a group, would lie about the whole thing, revisionists suggest that they would if they had a better understanding of the motivation. Some deniers believe that financial compensation was used to motivate the act.

Even today, Jewish families continue to receive enormous monetary compensation due to their loved ones' deaths or suffering. People all over the globe would view them as victims since they have already suffered enough hardships. They would therefore be entitled to treatment.

If the Holocaust was a hoax, how can it be that so many people have been duped?

People do not like getting fooled. It's possible that a person will never remember you as a fool if they see you standing next to someone who lied. Most people have a "detector" in their mind when it comes to determining truth and fabrication. How can you lie to the whole world and not be caught?

One sentence from a Chinese proverb sums it all: "A lie told a millionx will become truth." Perhaps, the Holocaust hoax was orchestrated by the most powerful Jewish groups to ensure favorable odds for the future.

Or, it could be that they weren't aware of the danger and realized how greedy Germans could be used against us. And the Jews seized the opportunity when it became available. No matter what reason there was for the deliberate plotting the revisionists knew full well that the gassing of Auschwitz camp residents was not real.

Verdict

The verdict is very much in favor of the believers. It states that the Holocaust was real and that the Nazis murdered approximately 6,000,000 Jews. This may make you wonder: how could that be possible when the Holocaust is a complete lie? Simple: More evidence is in the favors of the believers.

First of all, there was evidence in the first instance: 1,000,000 dead Jews were discovered in different pits. In addition to the corpses found in various pits, there were also documents prepared by those responsible for the mobile killer units. They had all of the death tolls as well as the details like how many men, women and children were killed.

The revisionists will claim that these documents are fake, but this is extremely unlikely. The reference markings on the documents corresponded to the German typewriters.

Second, these documents were found in numerous archives across Europe. Last, all the correct files were placed in the proper order. If the documents were faked, the Jews were able to complete the task in a very brief time.

These documents will not convince you. This is because deniers have been and continue to be looking for evidence that the Final Solution has been signed and ordered. You can't prove that thousands of documents were forged by the Jews - they could.

It should be simple - just one document needed to be placed in one archive for all to see. There was none of that document, whether it was fake or authentic.

The confessions. Deniers insist on the fact that those who confessed were subject to torture. Germans knew that they could be executed for their confessions so they would not have made them unless they were forced to. The statement of a person under duress was invalid.

Revisionists neglected to mention that most confessions were made after the defendants were sentenced. They would have died anyway so why did they confess? They weren't telling the truth.

The disappearances of thousands of Jews was, of course the strongest evidence that the Holocaust happened. Although this proof would be dismissed by many revisionists, it is still a strong argument that those Jews who went missing didn't die. They just migrated elsewhere, such as to the Soviet Union or United States. These countries already had a large Jewish population, so an additional couple million wouldn't make much difference.

In this light, deniers believed that those who disappeared did not re-connect with their prewar families because they had a bad (marriage) life.

While this was true, it isn't something that would happen to millions upon millions of Jews. Gassing busses was a real thing. So, at least that's what evidence shows. Dr. Herald Turner (chief of the German Administration of Serbia) wrote a letter to Karl Wolff, chief of Heinrich Himmler Personal Staff. He mentioned his plans to shoot any Jew he could. Later, he found a "delousingvan" that worked and hoped that they would be in a position to "clear camp" faster.

Another officer suggested that they could "improve” a bus's size. It would then be more maneuverable on roads and be less bulky when packed full of people.

It contained letters as well as physical evidence which showed that there had been gassing at the camps. There were also torture and an evident death wall. The Germans tried to cover up their tracks, which was true, but it was impossible due to the sheer volume of evidence.

Anne Frank's Diary was also examined. However, thorough investigations revealed that the entries had been authentic.

The Holocaust was a tragic historical event that was accepted by many people. This included the refugees who helped them and the ones who tried to help but couldn’t. Although the evidence is overwhelming for the authenticity of the Holocaust, it's comforting know that there are people willing and able to look into the matter because they are seeking the truth.

It doesn't really matter what the terrible events were, but it is undeniable that Holocaust is now part of world historical record.

Chapter 10: William Shakespeare isn't Real

https://en.wikipedia.org/wiki/William_Shakespeare#/media/File:Shakespeare.jpg

William Shakespeare, who was also a part of history, was behind many plays including Romeo & Juliet, Hamlet as well the Sonnets. He was well-known by many people. His books were reprinted a million more times than usual and his style of composing impressed both literary lovers and laymen. Some people think William Shakespeare wrote the famous plays.

We'll see how they came to that conclusion.

The movie Anonymous was released in several theaters recently. It was directed, among other things, by Roland Emmerich. Emmerich is the director of suspense films like Independence Day or The Day After Tomorrow. The film, which did not gain much popularity was about the possibility Shakespeare could have been written by someone else. According to the film Edward De Vere (17th Earl of Oxford), an aristocrat who served Queen Elizabeth I, wrote the plays.

But it does not necessarily mean Edward De Vere was only one candidate. There could have been many others who could be the author behind Shakespeare's most famous works. While there were many authors that were considered, Edward De Vere (Francis Bacon) and Christopher Marlowe made it to the list due to the "proof", as we will see later. Many people are surprised to learn that there are more than 50 candidates.

This Shakespeare denial does not rely solely on the film. In fact the confusion about William

Shakespeare's authenticity has been ongoing since almost two centuries. It was probably because of the lack evidence that Shakespeare actually existed.

Did you realize that William was only one of two portraits excepted from Anne Hathaway's marriage record, few signatures, and a 3-page will? In addition, business transaction records were kept to prove William was a real human being. What's more the business records didn't even have a connection to writing. It was not possible to find any record of schooling or manuscripts.

Shakespeare's authorship was doubted at times by celebrities, such as Henry James, Charlie Chaplin, Mark Twain and Sigmund Fréud. Mark Twain asserted that Shakespeare was "never wrote a single play in his entire life", while Henry James believed that the "Divine William" was the biggest, most successful fraud in our patient universe.

If Shakespeare was a fraud and Sigmund was right, perhaps Freud was just as accurate when he said that "such a shame" is not knowing who wrote the great tragedies, comedies, or sonnets.

We have the proof

1) The first, and most reliable proof was that Shakespeare wasn't a playwright. You can be honest and say that evidence suggests that the documents belonged a William Shaxpere or William Shaxpere. He was born in Stratford-upon-Avon. If you run into an academic scholar, and they mention William Shakespeare, remember that they are speaking about the actor, and not the playwright.

Records reveal that Shaksper's parents John, and Mary were illiterate. Even Anne Hathaway's wife was also illiterate. Even their children were anilliterate. If this actor was truly the man behind theatricals, then he'd be the only writer famous who didn't mind the literacy of their children.

Shaksper also never had any records of his schooling. To put it bluntly: it was as if Shaksper wasn't writing; Voltaire had thousands upon hundreds of letters and correspondence while William Shaxper only had one.

2) The second piece is the fact that the name "Shakes-spear," was a very popular nom-de–plume. People liked to use this penname back then, as it represented Pallas Athena, the Greek Goddess that always wore a sword. Shakespeares were also credited with works such as The London Prodigal. The Puritan. The Birth of Martin. The Comedy of George Greene.

What does this mean? It just means that Shakespeares were plentiful back then. It was possible that another author wrote his plays.

3) Third, Shakespeare's vast vocabulary. Shakespeare's Canon included more than 29,000 words. He is the only man to have the most English words. Did you realize that Paradise Lost by John Milton contained only 8,000 words? And then there's the Holy Bible. This was translated by 48 great British Biblical Scholars.

How could a single person, with no evidence of formal education, be capable of using 29,000 English terms with coherence.

4) Mark Twain tried to prove that William Shakespeare was not real in his work "Is Shakespeare Dead?" by explaining why no one had lamented the death the Bard of Stratford. According to Mark Twain, there was no sound in England at all when Shaxper died. Mark Twain wondered how this was possible. Does this mean that Shaxper wasn't a well-known playwright or was he? If he had been, there would have surely been poetry, memoirs, and tributes to the man responsible for creating heart-wrenching, moving plays. Mark Twain made this statement based on the fact other celebrated writers, such as Walter Raleigh or Francis Bacon, were appreciated at the moment of their deaths.

Conclusion? Shakespeare didn't write these famous plays.

5) His odd will. His bizarre will. The will was handwritten by his attorney. This would be surprising as a writer one would expect him to

do it, but it was done by his attorney. Second, he didn't mention anything about writing. If Stratford was passionate about his work, he would have probably included information about who would take care of the manuscripts. The last point is that someone as educated as William Shakespeare could possess hundreds of books. It would be reasonable to assume that he would protect them by including them into his will.

Was it because he didn't have any books, that he didn't include them in the will? For many, this was possible. It was believed that authorities would find the books. Authorities searched every bookcase within 50-miles of Stratford.

6) Did your know that William Shakespeare was fluent and proficient in several languages other then English? The fluency of the playwright in French (and Spanish, Spanish, German and Greek) was well-known. How was it possible for William Shaxper to learn all these languages in spite of being surrounded by illiterate people?

This proof has been established. Now we can move on to the other possible candidates. These people might be William Shakespeare.

Sir Francis Bacon

Sir Francis Bacon is one the qualified candidates. Sir Francis Bacon could have written the plays if he had studied at Cambridge and been a frequent traveler. Sir Francis Bacon was not only a philosopher but was also an active member of the Privy Council. He held the title of Lord-Chancellor.

Delia Bacon was the original person to suggest Sir Francis Bacon's name as the possible Bard -- there is no relationship. Delia Bacon, a Delia Bacon fan announced Francis Bacon to be the alternative author. Most people still doubt Shakespeare's authenticity. However, she claimed that he couldn't have written all those plays on his own. Instead, he must have worked with other prominent authors like Sir Walter Releigh & Edmund Spencer.

Delia replied when Delia was asked why they had to hide who they were. She claimed that the codes in the plays were meant to reproach the government for not taking immediate action on the disturbing issues of society.

Christopher Marlowe

Christopher Marlowe is a well-known playwright. His works, when compared to William Shakespeare, had many similarities in their style and patterns. The computer and humans made this comparison.

Marlowe also had a biography that suggested he was a spy serving the Crown. This gave him reason to hide his identity. People eventually discovered that Marlowe died in a scuffle in 1593. William Shakespeare continued to publish his works until 1614.

What could he have done after death to write if he was The Bard? Christopher Marlowe's followers turned the tables by using this "death," to their advantage. He fled and then continued to write plays.

Marlowe's candidacy was revealed as Shakespeare in a 2002 documentary called Much Ado About Something.

Edward De Vere

Edward De Vere was an unsuccessful candidate. However, for the past ninety years his supporters raised convincing arguments so that they were known as the Oxfordians. These Oxfordians were then the most challenging "enemies" of the Stradfordians. They are those who strongly believe that William Shakespeare wrote his original work.

J.T Looney (pronounced Loney), raised the idea for the first time. Following the 1920 publication of Shakespeare Identified, thousands of supporters sprung up, including prominent personalities such as Sigmund Fréud.

The Oxfordians suggested that Edward is the right choice since most Shakespeare plays include "legal" discussions. He was also a seasoned traveler. His experiences are reflected in Shakespeare's works.

Hamlet, the protagonist of the famous play Hamlet, described himself as "set nude" in the kingdom by some buccaneers after he encountered them. This scenario was similar with Edward De Vere's kidnapping. According to legend, the Earl was captured by pirates while traveling through the English Channel. He was then left naked in Denmark Shore. Let's not forget Hamlet being "The Prince" of Denmark.

A further interesting "proof", was the presence Rosencrantz or Guildernstern. These two were Hamlet's childhood friend, summoned from King Claudius to discover the reason for the prince's madness. If possible, they help stop it.

Guess what? De Vere's brother, in-law, apparently wrote him a note, detailing how he went to a banquet with two Courtiers named Rosencrantz and Guildernstern. According to Oxfordians, the very letter was private correspondence.

Oxfordians believe Hamlet is a play about Elizabethan Court. De Vere also believes this. Many characters actually resemble real life people. Polonius, for instance, was William Cecil, Lord Burghley and the trusted advisor of Elizabeth I. This character was also a reflection on Queen Gertrude.

Also, it's important to remember that Hamlet was involved with Polonius and Ophelia in the play. Guess what? It was Anne Cecil's daughter who married Edward De Vere in real life.

Many Oxfordians believe Hamlet to be an autobiographical piece that was created by the Earl in Oxford to expose the Elizabethan Court's activities. De Vere was accused of treason and the play itself was made to hide his identity. They pointed out that DeVere would have died if his pen name was not used.

William Shakespeare

Let's not forget those Stratfordians that believe Shakespeare wrote Shakespeare. They admit that William Shakespeare might have had to write some of his work on his own, and that he may have collaborated with other writers. But this does not alter the fact William Shakespeare was actually real.

They acknowledged that there was a serious lack of evidence regarding Shakespeare's schooling. But they also stated that anyone who studied in Stratford had the same issue. The absence of documentation does not necessarily indicate that there was no schooling.

This argument got the Stradfordians shamed. Some disbelievers thought they were holding onto an unreal thing to be able to continue living off Shakespeare's birth and life.

Shakespeare fans will argue about one thing. It is that Shakespeare's works, though a little unsubstantial in weight, are impossible to credit to anyone else. You can't really watch his works being credit to other men if he has invested his whole life into them.

Which theory do you believe? What theory appeals to the most to YOU?

Chapter 11: Most Famous Govt Cover Ups

The government is full of secrets. Some are only known by very high-ranking officials in the military or government. There is a reason for this secrecy. Certain developments and occurrences should not be revealed to foreign intelligence. This allows a government to maintain its military and strategic edge and ensure safety for all citizens. This does not mean that all facts can be shared with country residents. They are hidden, and this creates suspicions or paranoia.

President John F Kennedy

This is, undoubtedly, the most famous conspiracy theory. John F. Kennedy (the thirty-fifth president of the United States of America) was shot while riding in the parade in Dallas. It was already half past twelve when Kennedy was shot. His wife was also there. Police investigations were conducted for every murder. A Warren Commission investigation followed, which took ten months. The Warren Commission finally announced that John F. Kennedy, who was shot by Lee Harvey Oswald was the gunman. Jack Ruby killed the killer while Jack was being held for the murder. These findings were confirmed by further investigations.

Official findings reveal that the killer was believed to have fired three times. He was found at the Texas Book Depot, which overlooks where the president had been shot. The footage that emerged soon after the shooting showed the presidential vehicle and the plaza. One of the most intriguing things about these shots is that at minimum one was fired from an entirely different area. The bullet hitting its target can show this. Unfortunately, the 1960s footage quality was not great. This makes it difficult and impossible to confirm the number of shots actually fired. Many witnesses on the scene are certain they heard shots from the grass hills that overlook the plaza, according to testimony. This area may have had another gunman hiding behind a picket border.

It's hard to prove as conspiracy theories are difficult to prove. The film evidence has grainy details that make it difficult to determine which way. Official investigations have dismissed extra gunshots as echos, panic, and disorientation following the shock of the events.

To fuel the flames, the House Select Committee on Assassinations (the HSCA), conducted an investigation of both the FBI investigation, and the Warren commission report. Both were found to have been poorly done and to have a high chance of error. The HSCA confirmed it was likely at least four shots were fired. However it was difficult to tell if any of those firing were returning fire to the gunman. There have been several additional investigations into the HSCA report since 1979. Many have questioned its accuracy and questioned the conclusions of the HSCA. Needless to mention, this is still one of the most intriguing conspiracy theories of all.

The Moon Landings

It was the first time a human has been on the moon that the great space race took place in the history of mankind. NASA spent a huge amount of effort building a rocket capable enough to launch into space, land on a moon and return astronauts safely home. The US won the race. Neil Armstrong stepped onto space in front the cameras, while the rest of world watched. Many are fondly aware of his simple words, "One tiny step for man. One giant leap for humanity."

However, one theory suggests that the moon landers were not real. The theories range from astronauts filming the landings at a secret Hollywood location or in desert locations to a simpler theory that the astronauts altered the photos and documents they sent back to make it look like the astronauts actually landed on Mars. These theories stress the fact that moon landings were possible because of a technological leap that was almost impossible at the time. Humankind had barely reached the moon by the 1960's. To ensure America won the race for space, America had to be secretive, just like with other government projects.

Other theories include the possibility that the shadows in some of the photographs were inaccurate or that Buzz Aldrin moved the flag incorrectly on the Moon. This simple explanation is that, despite all science advancements and the current knowledge about space, it is impossible to predict how anything will react in space. Even the number stars in the background can be questioned.

There are even more extreme theories that a human footprint and skeleton could have been found on the moon. But this is not possible because the moon doesn't have any atmosphere. It makes it impossible for bodies to decompose. Despite this impossibility, the theory is still being promoted and provides credibility to those who believe that the moon landings may have been faked. However, all investigations and leading scientists have confirmed that the moon landers were real. The theories however continue.

The theory now suggests that there could be a space fleet operating outside of Earth's orbit. This fleet is related to both the Department of Defence, and the UN. However, it has not been explained what its purpose is.

The Illuminati

This is one of most popular conspiracies. It simply states that there have been several very powerful and secretive organizations who are planning to control all humanity with one organization. The plan's main driver has been identified as being the Illuminati. This group intends to create the New World Order. Even though it seems unlikely that countries would want this, the secret parties are made up of high ranking officials.

This group uses a variety of methods to achieve their goals. They use finance, political leverage and other resources to slowly control the world. One of the most important beliefs is the fact that the group has the ability to use mind control to force certain people to do their will. They also publish a great deal of material that isn't knowingly connected to them. However, this keeps people afraid of particular consequences and ensures that they get the reaction they want.

The conspiracy theorists propose that the United Nations, US government, European

Union, IMF, World Bank, NATO and NATO all are part of this new order.

The power to control the thoughts and actions of people is held by large government agencies and other big institutions. This can be done simply by putting the right information at their fingertips and suppressing anything else. It is sometimes necessary to preserve order and civilised life. However, this also confirms the idea of one global government. However, there may be tensions and wars all over the globe that counteract this. The conspiracy theorists also show the Illuminati's capability to influence and direct mankind by converting real money to electronic funds. It will become impossible to control or see your funds any more. All funds can eventually be made electronic so that one group can easily manage them. This theory suggests some of world's most important banks and bankers are involved. This is evidence that this conspiracy is on a large scale.

It is even suggested that wars can be started and attacks and apparent natural catastrophes are caused by attempts to manipulate the population into agreeing with the organisation's goals. Another example is the idea that the one government would control everything by controlling microchips. The theory also suggests that the headquarters for this new order might be in an underground metropolis below Denver Airport. It is much larger than an ordinary city airport and lies at a distance that is unusually far from the city.

However, evidence is lacking for these theories at this point.

Jesus

This concept will be familiar to anyone who's ever heard, read, or seen The Da Vinci Code. Most people accept the fact Jesus existed. This theory however goes further than the others and claims that Jesus was married to Mary Magdalene and had kids with her, before he died. Mary and her kids fled to Southern France shortly after the execution. There they married various noblemen who eventually made their family the Merovingian clan. The idea is that secret documents may be available to verify this claim. This secret society could have access to such documents. This secret society kept this secret for thousands years and will continue to do it until the rightful heir is placed on the throne. This is something the royals and current government do not want us to know.

The conspiracy theory goes further than that. It also believes the church deliberately kept these documents hidden because they confirmed that Jesus was a male and that the entire Christian Church is built upon an incorrect belief. In its efforts to hide this information, church has grown bigger and more powerful. The church now has a significant impact on all local governments, schools and other decisions. It is unlikely that the church has been implicated in clandestine actions, though it has a chequered past.

Watergate

This incident dates back from 1972. It began June 17th with four burglars trying to break into National Democratic Committee. The unusual thing about the four burglars was that they were all dressed in smart clothes. Nixon's demise was precipitated by the scandal.

According to some theories, Nixon's involvement was confirmed by evidence found at the National democratic Committee. It is possible that the Paris peace discussions would have failed without the help of Nixon's team. The evidence found was in the form illegal wire taps. This evidence wasn't found. It did, however, lead to the FBI's investigation into the break-in in order to uncover a connection between Mexican bank accounts and the Plumbers.

The Plumbers was a codename of a group that President Nixon created to assist him. They were primarily ex CIA agents that operated solely under the White House. Their mission was to locate information on opposing democrats. They were created because the FBI wouldn't stop them from investigating the links between Mexican bank and Plumbers. In fact, it ordered the CIA to end any FBI investigation into Watergate funds.

Mark, the second-in command of the FBI felt he was leaking details to the media. He was eventually confronted and resigned. The subject of conspiracy theories and debate is the level of involvement of President Nixon, whether Felt was a patriotic American or a disgruntled FBI employee who tried to get their back against Nixon.

The Princess and Prince of Wales

Charles and Diana had the fairytale wedding of their dreams and a perfect marriage. The wedding was ultimately a failure, and the princess moved on to her own life. She became a loved national figure, eventually falling in love with Dodi Faley, the son the luxury department and famous department store Harrods. The theory is that the British government was concerned about how a marriage between them would affect the British monarchy. To stop this happening, a plot to kill Diana was devised.

According to theory, a white Fiat Uno (white car) was driven into the tunnel at night 1997. The Fiat was designed to blind and distract the driver of Diana's car. Henri Paul (the driver) was already speeding when he was being pursued and photographed by hundreds eager to capture a photo of Diana. This added distraction resulted in the crash that claimed the lives of Dodi as well as Diana. Some theories even suggest that Henri Paul was even able to switch his blood alcohol level so it indicated that he had exceeded the legal limit for drink driving.

Despite the theory persisting for many years, however, the official investigation proved it was an unfortunate accident. They also found no evidence that anyone else was involved in their death.

It's also worth noting, that while Diana was alive she could have been a threat the British Monarchy and possibly the government. However when she was dead, there were far more questions about whether it was an accident. The British monarchy suffered for many years under a dark cloud. But that cloud has now been lifted and the new generation is showing their determination for life as both royals, and people.

The list is endless of government cover-ups. You will find almost every conspiracy theory linked to the government. It is almost a given that the government is the easiest target and most likely to be covered up. It does not mean that all theories are right. Each one must be evaluated for its merits before you can decide.

Chapter 12: Global Warming, The Greatest Conspiracy.

Global warming is a concept that most people have encountered. Global warming is believed to be caused by the increase in pollution and other environmental effects humans have on the earth. Research suggests that global warming is caused by humans. Particularly, this could be due to the excessive burning of fossil fuels. Normal process of nature absorbs carbon dioxide and then releases it into the atmosphere. Humanity, as a human race, produces two times as much carbon dioxide today as any existing plant in the world. The result is that the atmosphere is becoming flooded with carbon dioxide.

This will lead to a rise in ocean temperatures that can have an adverse effect on the icecaps. The warmer water can stop as much ice being formed at each icecap and can even melt some of existing ice. The result is an imbalance within nature. The result is an imbalance in nature. A smaller ice cap means more water, higher levels of seawater and the possibility that low-level land could become flooded. These greenhouse gases trap heat within the earth, which causes the planet's temperature to rise. This will lead to an increase in sea levels. It will also increase the amount of precipitation that occurs and the number of storms that occur. It is possible to see an increase in extreme weather events, such as flash floods and thunder storms. These extreme events can make it difficult to live a normal life and could also cause irreversible damage.

Carbon dioxide is making the problem worse because it remains in our atmosphere. This is because it prevents heat from the sun and hot water from leaving our planet. NASA has kept records for one hundred, thirty-four years on the average temperature. It has been increasingly evident that the average global temperature is increasing. These numbers show that temperature has increased faster than it has in the past eighty four year. Since 2000, fifteen of 16 hottest year ever recorded are actually from this year.

There is growing concern about global warming. Although it was initially dismissed as a fiction, people are becoming more concerned about global warming and what it might mean for the planet. It is important to reduce emissions from individuals and industries. This has been discussed by governments all over the world. It is not surprising that many of the largest companies in the world have put in a lot of effort to achieve this goal. Each of these companies is adhering with government guidelines, which aim at gradually reducing the production of harmful carbon dioxide. It is also interesting that global warming can be attributed to the long droughts experienced in California during 2015, and for stronger tropical storms. This could be due to warmer seas. Global warming can be attributed even to the latest spate of massive storms and hurricanes which have caused widespread damage around the globe.

Global warming is not just going to cause a warmer Earth or more severe storms. As scientists learn more about the effects heat has on the earth, it has become apparent that there will soon be an increase water shortages and risk for fires in certain areas and a contrast increase in flooding elsewhere. Floods are likely affecting all aspects of farming. Fishing industry and other industries will be affected. Farmers will also need to deal more with pests. There will be an increase in pollen and an increase in the incidence of infectious diseases.

Global warming is an issue that has received a lot of attention. It can also be influenced by how we can reduce them. There was little evidence when the concept was first made. It was a theory that was more important than scientific fact. This led many conspiracy theories to be born.

Financial Gain

The main reason any conspiracy theory exists is that it suggests someone will profit financially from the planned action. This is one of many conspiracy theories that arose after the global warming claims. Already there has been much talk about the short supply of oil remaining and how crucial it is to life as we know it. To reduce consumption and increase profit for all the parties, whether Russian or American billionaires and Middle East Oil suppliers, a propaganda drive was launched that will justify the increasing prices and taxes on these precious fuels. Extremist groups, which depend on oil profits, can generate this type information.

The theory holds that there is no increase of carbon dioxide in our atmosphere. Even if there is, it doesn't have any effect on the Earth's temperature. It is a naturally occurring, organic gas that is found in the atmosphere. The amounts can change from one time to the next. In reality, the Earth's temperature is dropping. This is why the research is only helping the most wealthy people on Earth become more prosperous.

There are many facts to support this theory. These can include:

* Global warming can be assumed to be happening. There is no way to know if it is human-caused or natural. It's possible for the earth to go through cycles with warmer and colder periods. Although the last ice-age was many years ago, it's difficult to determine if global heat fluctuations over extended periods of time. There has been even speculation that this could be a natural cooling period after the four hundred-year cooling period known by the little iceage.

* A majority of the carbon dioxide that is found in the atmosphere is due to natural causes like the ocean and plants. It's hard for us to believe that just three or four per cent of the atmosphere's carbon dioxide is created by humans.

* Most of the gases that are found in the air, commonly called greenhouse gases, are just water vapour. Only around 4 percent of these gases contain carbon dioxide. In other words, carbon dioxide emitted and absorbed by the Earth is less than 1 percent of the atmosphere. Even with such delicate infrastructure, it is hard to accept that human contributions to this atmosphere can make a significant difference. This is also evident by the fact that humans have little effect on temperature. According to some reports, a reduction of carbon dioxide that is human-produced by 30% could reduce the temperature by just one twentieth degree.

* The current phase, which began in 1850 and continues to this day, has seen no significant shift in the momentum of global warming. It's only experienced a small increase each of these years.

The most concerning thing is that carbon dioxide levels are rising and caused the global heat index to drop by 0.75% in 2007/2008. This effect rebalanced the warming that occurred in the 100 years preceding it.

* Although the data available is very limited, it doesn't appear that there's a strong correlation between the temperature on the Earth and the carbon dioxide released over the period. Unfortunately, it is not possible to assess whether the overall carbon dioxide levels for these years were significantly lower or higher than any other time. Recent studies have shown an increase carbon dioxide levels in the atmosphere, since 1995. However there is no statistical evidence for global warming.

This fact is confirmed by the Hadley Centre that is part of UK Met office.

* There is approximately 3000 robots that constantly monitor the temperature of the ocean and report back to NASA. Unfortunately, these robots show that the sea's temperature is actually declining.

* Nearly six thousand boreholes around the world have been created. These data have given us a wealth of information about the past and present of the earth. These statistics indicate that the Medieval Warm era saw temperatures three degrees higher on average than the current world temperatures. This is also supported today by the fact glaciers in the Andes that were not present in Medieval Warm. This makes it clear that even a three degree rise is significant, which is far more than many global warming theories claim. Even the Viking settled on Greenland in areas that are nearly always covered by permafrost. In fact, the Chinese fleet of navy boats that

sailed around North Pole in 1941 were seen sailing around it.

* The Antarctic Ocean appears to have become much colder than it was thirty years ago and has gained ice. This is quite a contrast to all six thousand years prior. More evidence points towards an impending glacier age than a global cooling.

* Scientists have found that the atmospheric carbon dioxide levels during Paleoclimatological periods were significantly higher than they are today. In fact, these levels are among the lowest in over five hundred fifty million years.

* Mars, which is expected to be colonized by humans in the next fifteen years, is an interesting and relevant fact. The atmosphere of this planet is almost ninety% carbon dioxide. But, it has a temperature that ranges from 0 to over one hundred degrees Celsius. This suggests that carbon

dioxide in the atmosphere has little impact on the planet's temperatures.

* Scientists and other scientists have different views on global warming. Over 32,000 scientists have signed a petition declaring that the human impact on global warming is negligible.

* There is extensive research on the impact of temperature changes and carbon dioxide levels. The vast majority of research on carbon dioxide levels and temperature changes concludes that the temperature is changing first, and carbon dioxide second. It has even been demonstrated that carbon dioxide levels can rise hundreds years after temperatures have increased. This shows that temperature is the main driver of carbon dioxide. However, they are not independent. Therefore, human carbon dioxide production won't have any impact on Earth's temperature.

* Many scientific predictions of how climate will change over the next fifty year are based in part on the same computer program that predicts the weather. This software has a rate of error of forty four percent. Nearly half (48%) of the weather forecasts are inaccurate, so there's no reason to have faith in long-term predictions. It is impossible for a computer to accurately predict weather conditions for more than seven days. How will it be able forecast 50 or 100 years down the line?

Global warming is possible but is not necessarily a good thing. Many theories suggest the increase in size of the dinosaurs could be attributed to the warm climate and abundant food. These were times when carbon dioxide levels had been much higher than they currently are. It's also worth noting the fact that more people die in warm environments than when they live in colder areas.

* Greenland's Ice Cores show that the earth is constantly changing. Each phase takes approximately 1 000 5 hundred years. At the moment, we are likely in a heating cycle. This is what the ice cores have shown for the last four hundred and thousand years. This makes sense because the Earth cannot maintain a perfect temperature at all times. There is too much to consider. It is natural to assume that the earth will either be cooling or heating. These phases are likely to last for many years, since the planet has been here for billions. We've always known about the problem of cooling and warming, but haven't had the technology to fully assess it.

* Increased carbon dioxide can help plants produce more crops. A rich carbon dioxide environment will result in large fruits and vegetables that require minimal intervention. This is the nature of the earth. Global warming will be natural and productive if the temperature fluctuates as

it should. It will also help plants to grow where they are presently unable.

* Global temperature rises were predicted by the IPCC. The IPCC has shown that the current global temperature is not reaching the bottom of the forecasts. This shows how far out the data are.

* Sunspots are more likely to affect the Earth's temperature than any human carbon dioxide production. The number sunspots has been falling over the last tenyears, which suggests that a mini glacier may be in the making.

Scientists will argue that there are many facts that can be used to refute or support the principle of global cooling. To most people, it's just data on a graph. It's impossible to prove or demolish the data. One thing is certain: while the governments are benefiting from higher taxes, the oil richest billionaires around the world are also benefiting. This could be a link to the Illuminati conspiracy theory.

Chapter 13: Aliens - Are They Already With Us?

It is inevitable that UFO's, aliens, or government cover-ups are discussed when discussing conspiracy theories. It is the ultimate, unanswered question of the universe. Are aliens real? As we spend more time looking at the universe, it becomes increasingly obvious that there is a lot more star systems and planets than Earth. It is becoming more unlikely that humans would be the only ones in the universe. However, because some of these worlds are older, it begs the question why some civilisations haven't yet connected to Earth. If their technology has advanced at an equal rate, they should be able fly in space.

It is possible for some of these species to have no interest or desire in crossing vast distances, or they may not be willing to invest the financial resources necessary. However, it seems that at least some of these creatures will be able to have the same persistence as humans and have the same curiosity, which suggests that they will continue the long trek to Earth along with many other planets.

It is logical to assume that life exists on other planets. If so, then there are two options. One is that the aliens don't want us to interrupt our own progress; the other is they may have already made contact with Earth. Many theories exist about aliens visiting Earth, UFO sightings, or aliens living amongst humans. However, if an alien has been seen on the planet already and is currently living there, then it would mean that their appearance is very similar to a human. The question now is whether this is true. It's possible, but it's unlikely. Certainly, if the alien species is from a similar planet to earth, they will have likely developed in the same way. This does not support many of the assumptions about aliens. For example, the notion that they have larger heads in order to house their larger brains is a natural part of evolution.

Roswell

This is one conspiracy theory that is well-known and most widely known. It is more than seventyyears old. Roswell AFB released a press announcement in 1947 that claimed they had found a mysterious, silver-colored disc on a nearby ranch. After realizing their mistake, the Roswell Air Force Base personnel released a press release claiming that they had found a mysterious silver metallic disc on a ranch near the base. But the media had already noticed the potential and began to publish front-page stories suggesting they had found an extraterrestrial space craft. The story quickly grew into several stories about crashed alien craft. In fact, they even recovered two bodies. The subsequent footage of an alien autopsy was revealed to have been at least partially faked. This made it impossible for the evidence to be authentic.

Roswell is a secret training and test facility that has a large area restricted to traffic, which led to the speculation that aliens were found. The government accidentally fueled the rumours by giving Area 51 a code name. This name implied that the government was trying to hide something and that these stories were true. There are many stories to this day about the airbase, alien craft, aliens, and the development new technologies.

Most conspiracy theorists claim that the government is hiding the existence, or trying to hide it since the date of the alien encounter. However, others argue that it might be correct to do this in order to stop panic. Many people will be affected by alien life. Is it possible for humans to learn from the alien species?

Phoenix

On the 13th March 1997, six lights were seen across the city. According to reports the lights moved slowly along the horizon before moving on to a row of eight lights. After the second row, a third row of ten lamps followed. All three rows were in the standard V formation. There were five more reports from Arizona. These reported came from different cities. They all followed the same flight route and all of them said the exact same thing. The sightings took place over four hours. Phoenix was first to see the lights at 10:30 pm. Other cities had left by 2am.

There have been two other instances of lights over Phoenix: in 2007 as well as 2008. The government has not provided any explanations beyond that it could be flares being dropped on the ground or helium balls with flares attached. But, this was never made clear. A few residents claimed that three jets belonging to the air force flew over the skies during the 2008 incident, probably heading towards the city lights. The air force, however, denies there being any planes in air that day. The governor dismissed the notion of alien craft at first, but he later said that the aliens looked distinct.

Minais Gerais

This incident is known as the Varginha matter. According to reports, it took place in January 1996. Witnesses saw a shapeless submarine in the sky about twenty feet from the ground. Witnesses claimed that the craft wasn't working properly. The local residents reported seeing multiple beings in the village the next morning. According to some reports, one of them was shot dead and another taken to the hospital. According to an interview with an orthopedic surgeon, the creatures were five feet tall and had very thin necks. Although they seemed dry to the touch, it was clear that they needed to be wet.

Apart from the many witnesses, there was also a reported leakage of information from an officer of Brazil's air force. According to the source, NORAD alerted CINDACTA about a possibility of a UFO landing in south Minas Gerais. Local authorities have never commented on this incident. A witness claimed to have witnessed the military rounding up the individuals and loading the craft onto a truck. However again, no proof has ever emerged.

UFO's

If this story is true, then it would be reasonable to assume that aliens can navigate around Earth. This would be supported by the many UFO sightings that happen every year. If you examine the right papers, you will see UFO sightings happening every week. Many sightings can easily be explained by schedule flights, unusual weather patterns, or any number of other reasons. There are always exceptions to the rule. These incidents help conspiracies grow and become part legend.

Many high ranking personnel have declared aliens are present:

Paul Hellyer

This man was once Canada's defence minister. He spent many years researching the issue of alien life. He has declared publicly that he believes there are aliens and that there has not been enough cover up by the US Government. He believes part of the reason is the rapid advance in technology over fifty years. He believes this was due to experts reverse-engineering alien technology.

According to some reports, he spent hours analyzing all evidence and testimonials to decide which is true. He concludes that it is possible to prove that UFOs are real, and that any person who has witnessed one is genuine.

Karl Wolf

Karl was an electronic photographer and precision electronics repairman in the air force. In his spare time, he was assigned to the lunar orbiter project that NASA was managing at Langley. He was working on the damaged equipment when the operator abruptly told him that they found a base at the back of the moon. The operator then showed him some photographs. Each photo included a collection either of mushroom-shaped buildings or spherical buildings. Karl didn't know how to react and he kept quiet because he was afraid he would be hurt if he tried to ask any more questions.

Donna Hare

Donna was an illustrator and designer as an employee of the firm that supplied NASA. This allowed Donna to see confidential items. Donna's work was crucial in landing and launch slides. One tech showed Donna an image showing Earth with a dot. Donna assumed it was a spot in the camera or similar. The tech then explained that it would not create shadows on Earth. The tech said that the image would then be airbrushed before anyone could see.

Edgar Mitchell

This former astronaut is the only one to have ever walked onto the moon. He believes that aliens watch the earth constantly. He cites the evidence that he saw and the fact of so many stars in our universe that it would seem impossible that there is not another form life. He is happy to admit that he hasn't seen an alien. However, he believes the people who have told him that they are right. This gives him credibility despite his government officials stating that he's a decent man, but that he has wandered a bit. His claim that he saw them isn't true, but that he did see some evidence shows that he is credible.

Sightings

Apart from the beliefs of these people, there are numerous instances which lend credence to the theory of alien life.

* In 1947, William Rhodes took pictures of an unusual flying object that flew over Arizona. The photographs were published in local publications, sparking speculation about secondary sightings. The FBI and a soldier of the army's air force intelligence stole the negatives.

The Air Force UFO reporting classified reveals that the negatives were seized by an army air force intelligence officer and the FBI. A further explanation was never given.

Donald Keyhole, an ex-Marine and UFO expert, was seen on TV in 1958. He knew what he was allowed and could not say. When he tried straying from the agreed script, the sound was instantly cut. The network explained that they were forced to remove the sound because it would have been against security standards. No further explanation was provided, leaving those who believe it to be alien conspiracy theory to conclude that he was just about to confirm alien existence and that they were already active throughout the entire plant. It is believed that his research and earlier comments hinted at this possibility and that this was the obvious conclusion for his followers.

* John Callahan, 1986 Federal Aviation Authority. He was the chief of the accident-investigations branch. He reported a Boeing 747 spotting a UFO in Alaska. The pilots of the plane reported seeing an object move along with

them for several kilometers and asked the tower to verify. The tower confirmed the object could be seen on radar, but they didn't know its exact nature. Following protocols, the aviation board began an investigation. Callahan talked with the presidents of scientific study groups and other officers. This included a CIA agent. Callahan was advised by a CIA operative not long after the meeting that they weren't there. That was it. The CIA did not want public hysteria.

There are many other examples of people who believe they have seen or heard something of alien origin. While some people will simply shrug off the situation and carry on their lives, others will change their tune and allow the story to take them where they want. It is difficult without the evidence to prove what you saw; it can make you look paranoid.

There has been an explosion in aliens, space, and general interest since the International Space Station's most recent mission. NASA has been collecting pictures from Mars as well as Jupiter. These new theories have led to other conspiracies and theories, but what's more interesting is the diversity of alien lifeforms that have been discussed in discussions by those who had seen them. Despite all of these sightings they still have no proof they exist.

Greys

These are divided into three types

1. Four foot tall humanoids featuring large heads, slanting eyes and large heads.

2. Although four feet tall, the humanoid also has three fingers and a slightly smaller, more angular forehead.

3. These greys are four feet tall.

The Nordics

These were named due to their similarity in appearance to the Swedish. They often have blond hair and are slightly shorter than the average individual.

Shape Shifters

As their names suggest, they can adjust their shape to match the environment. Nobody seems to know whether this applies to living or immaterial objects or if there is an limit to how many shapes they can adopt.

Short Humanoids

These animals are essential for human appearance, but much smaller than the average person at two feet.

While there are many different types of aliens that people have described on the internet, it is important to remember that all of these are humanoid. Many of them have the head of a typical alien photograph. This raises interesting questions about whether these pictures influence alien beliefs or whether they were influenced by aliens in their past. It would make sense to base our alien image on something we've seen before.

Whatever your belief, aliens are real. An increasing number of people claim they have seen them. However the question remains, "If these beings are capable to travel through space, how would they be content to remain secretive on Earth?"

Chapter 14: Unsolved Mysteries in the World

One thing is for sure, no matter what conspiracy theory you believe, nearly everyone will enjoy discussing it. The natural curiosity inherent in the human mind will undoubtedly make you curious as to what really happened. You won't be satisfied with a simple tale or a complex story.

This is the reason why so many conspiracy theories end up being proven false. If probed long enough and with enough effort, any mystery not solved will be solved. Despite this, there are still mysteries to be solved.

Aluminium Wedge

The edge of the Mures River in Romania was spotted a wedge-shaped block of aluminium alloy covered in a thin layer of oxide in 1974. The object was located about a mile away from Aiud.

The find is said that it was submerged in thirty feet of sand. It also had two mastodon bone bones nearby. It's interesting that this find was located next to the bones. This indicates that it is 11 000 years old. Aluminum was discovered only at the beginning 1800's. This suggests that either the bulk of the evidence was buried in the area to create the impression, but that it also dates from a time that humans would not have been capable of creating it.

It's impossible to know more about this alloy and its origins.

Babushka

Unknown facts about John F. Kennedy's assassination include the fact that a woman was standing next to his car when he was shot. While only the back of her can be seen in the numerous photos, she was wearing long brown clothes and a scarf made from babushka on her head. While it seems that she was holding the camera, it is not certain. She didn't leave the scene immediately after the killing. In fact, she was among the last to leave. She was seen going up Elm Street. Then she went to the east. Despite an FBI appeal, no one knows who she is and whether she was filming. Another mystery is still unsolved.

Marine Corp Air Crash

In 1993, four Marine Corp personnel were killed in a crash. The personnel were all on active duty and thought to be participating in friendly exercises. The accident scene was sealed off by government officials so that no member of the public could see. The helicopter was part on the presidential fleet. It was transporting only the marine corp. crew.

An investigation found that the crash was accidental. There's still lots of room to maneuver! Accidental can cover a pilot's death, a misjudgment, or even being struck by friendly fire while on a training exercise. Many people believe it was a friendly incident due to the complete silence. There is no clear answer.

Dighton Rock

The boulder at the Taunton River in Massachusetts is enormous, weighing in around forty tonnes. The boulder doesn't really look special until you approach it and realize it has petroglyphs. It was noticed for the first time over three hundred and fifty years ago. No one has ever been able understand their meaning.

In 1680, the first mention of the boulder was made by someone who had traveled from England in order to colonize the new lands. The government removed the boulder to preserve it. However, there are many theories regarding its origins. They include Native American, Portuguese and even ancient Phoenicians.

The Voynich manuscript

This manuscript, which is believed to have been written during the Middle Ages, uses a language unique to its time. There have been many attempts at figuring out the meanings of words and letters. But, none of them has succeeded. There are pictures of flowers within the book which may indicate it to be an alchemist's work. If this is the case, it's possible that the code he used was to keep his findings secret. There are many types of flower in the book which have never before been seen by modern botanists. However, the code will never be cracked so no one can find out what was in his books. It will continue being a challenge.

It is not easy to decode the book and also it is difficult to pinpoint its source. It is well-known that the book was purchased for six hundred golden ducats by Emperor Rudolph II. It is believed that he believed that Richard Bacon had written it. This is due to John Dee being the one who purchased the book. He also owned many Richard Bacon manuscripts. Jacobus de Tipenecz is believed to have received it. It is known that it was also given to Athanasius Churcher in 1666. In 1912, Wilfred M. Voynich purchased it from Jesuit College. H.P. H.P.

The Bermuda triangle

Although this isn't as frequent in the news now, it is still an area where pilots and sailors should avoid. It is located in the Western North Atlantic and covers large parts of the oceans. It is home to many mysterious disappearances of boats and aircrafts. It is located between Miami, Puerto Rico and Bermuda. Some people pass through this area daily without incident. Others disappear without a trace. A whole squadron US Navy bombers was reported to have become disorientated.

The Bermuda Triangle has been the scene of more incidents and disappearances than any other region of the sea. One thing that is unique is the large number of boats that disappear without communicating with their final destination and are never found. Though there are many possibilities, such as alien abduction or very bad weather, or even a portal that leads to another dimension, none have been proved.

Saint Germain

While this man seems to have been born in mid-1700's, there are hints that his birth may have occurred much earlier: around the time Christ was conceived! He is also believed to have been linked with prominent individuals as recently as 1970.

It is known that he worked as an alchemist. He was said to be able to transform almost any metal into golden; he also discovered the secret to eternal youth. He was a celebrity during the 1740's through the 1950's, 60's up to 70's up until the 1780s. He traveled extensively, was fluent in twelve languages, and was often quoted as being able even to speak twelve languages. He was also a talented violin player and a master painter. Although he seemed wealthy, there isn't evidence that he ever had one. Also, all the reports about him stating that he looked around forty five were accurate. He did not eat out with his friends, but he was known to enjoy eating oatmeal in private. His clothes were covered with jewels. According to legend, he was capable of painting and joining diamonds together. He was also a known member of many secret societies, including the Illuminati (Order of the Templars). He is believed he died in 1784. But he has been seen many other times since.

He was also seen with Anton Mesmerthe, the pioneer hypnotist, just one year later. He seems to have been selected by the Freemasonary that same year. Comtesse d'Adhemar stated that he appeared to her several times, most recently in 1820. He appeared each time after a significant event occurred, as he had said. It is unknown if he is still living or dead.

Jack the Ripper

This is without doubt the greatest known killer of all time. His reputation was built during the late 1800's. He was busiest in 1888. He was a gangster who primarily targeted prostitutes in London's Whitechapel neighbourhood. Bizarrely, despite several victims being found within minutes of their deaths, his identity was never revealed. This is because he is believed to have removed and mutilated organs from victims. And yet, he disappears right before the body is found.

Jack the Ripper is responsible for 11 murders. There could have been more, however. We don't know anything about Jack the Ripper, or who he is. Jack the Rifle was the name given to the case. It was the name used at the beginning of a letter that was forwarded at the time to the police. The police chose to make Jack the Ripper public. This added excitement, fear and intrigue to their murders.

The Shroud of Turin

This shroud was believed to have been used by Jesus after his crucification. Although the shroud's age has been determined and the fabric was available in Middle Ages, it is known that its existence dates back to the fourth-century, pre-modern Middle Ages. Its weave and pollen can be said to date it from the time Jesus was alive, which is also consistent with other fabrics of that period. However, the shroud contains an image showing a crucified man. The puzzle has remained, as no one has been able reproduce the image onto this material. The material shouldn't have existed, and yet it clearly came from the time Jesus. It also features a picture on which it is impossible for anyone to reproduce with current technology. This is one puzzle we may never solve.

Frederick Valentich

The young pilot was trying to get as many flying hours possible in his single engine aircraft. This would give him the opportunity to become a commercial flight instructor. On a fateful day, however, he flew just one-hundred and thirty miles from Melbourne over King Island. Twelve minutes after takeoff, his last contact was with Melbourne traffic police. He said he could spot four bright green lights above his head. He was only about 1000 feet away from the lights. He stated that the object seemed as if it were playing with his head, and was moving extremely fast between him and the object. The pilot ended his sentence with the words "It's not an airplane ". Unfortunately, the radio was cut off and Frederick Valentich could not be found again. His plane and pilot were never found, despite an extensive sea-air search.

Frederick's father confirmed that Frederick was interested in UFOs and that he had already reported seeing one 10 months prior to the incident. The police received several calls on the same evening reporting a sighting. The obvious explanation was that either his plane crashed due to the UFO or that he'd been kidnapped.

A further twist to this mystery was the sighting of Frederick in 1990. This was 12 years after his disappearance. He was spotted in Tenerife. He claimed he had been recruited alongside several other human beings by aliens. But he didn't specify what he had been trained to do.

He still looked the same as when he disappeared. Frederick has not returned since his disappearance, which is a mystery that may have alien connections.

Dyatlov Pass

Ten skiers were embarking on a dangerous trek. Nine of them lost their lives in extreme weather conditions. The incident took place on February 2, 1959. The diary entries of the participants provide most of the information. It was reported that some members of the group literally tore their tents out from the inside and walked off into night wearing only their bed clothes.

It took three days to find the bodies, which were located only a few hundred meter from the tents. The four remaining bodies were found two months later. These bodies were found with pieces of clothing that belonged previously to their owners. The radiation levels in the clothes they were wearing were confirmed by tests. Also, the bodies showed evidence of large-scale internal trauma. Some had fractured skulls and broken teeth. Bizarrely, a Russian investigator concluded that there was nothing to suggest foul play and closed off the investigation. The only member of this party that survived had been taken ill before the trek started and had remained in a nearby village.

The most chilling aspect of the tale is Ludmila Durbinina's second set of bodies, which was found with broken vertebrae and her tongue missing. The group appears to have suffered extensive internal injuries similar to a car wreck, but there was no external injury. There may have been many reasons for these events. However, Dubinina's removal and radioactive clothing were just a few of the clues. Also, the Russians quickly locked the files away. There were reports that flying spheres appeared in the area. It is unknown if these are Russian testing or alien-derived. The only thing that is certain is the inability to explain all radiation and injuries by an avalanche or hypothermia. Even a fall would not explain the appearance of one member returning to the camp. Although all records have been destroyed, the main investigator died.

Area 51

What is Area 51, exactly?

One detachment from Edwards Air Force Base is called Area 51. Area 51 is located approximately 85 miles northwest of Las Vegas and is part of the Edwards Air Force Base. The US Government is the owner of the area. It is currently operated by the US Air Force. Area 51's stated purpose is to test and develop prototype weapons and aircraft that will be used by US military forces. Area 51 is sometimes referred to as Dreamland (paradise ranch), Homey Airport (home base), and Dreamland. Military personnel use the terms “the box” and “the container” to refer to the restricted airspace within Area 51.

Why is it so fascinating?

Area 51 is attractive because of the secrecy that surrounds it. There is often a lot more secrecy in areas that are used to test and evaluate new aircraft and weaponry for the military. But, some believe that the shroud covering Area 51 could conceal even deeper secrets. One reason is that the US government rarely acknowledges the existence of the Base. They won't discuss it and don't address it.

Another reason people are interested in the mystery is the abundance of lights visible in the sky over Area 51. Many believe that the lights are due the weapon and aircraft production at the base. But, they are not convinced.

Military personnel were able to retrieve alien spaceships believed to have crashed in the vicinity. It is thought that most of the research and experimentation at the base involves technology not from Earth. However, they are heavily influenced by the alien craft that crashed on the site. According to some military scientists, they are trying reverse engineer alien technology for military use. They're not only looking at the craft, but also studying the occupants.

Area 51 is not just a place where technology engineering is done. Many believe there are strange things happening at Area 51. This is why secrecy and restrictions on airspace are necessary to protect those who are not privy to their presence.

Area 51 is also said to be studying other alien species. It is believed that the government has been using the space for technology development that would enable time travel and teleportation. They believe that the government has been working to control the weather for some time and could already be using that technology in the present.

Many of the weird happenings at Area 51 are related to the underground facilities at Papoose Lake/Groom Lake. People also believe that Area 51 has a transcontinental train that allows personnel to fast, secretly, travel across America. A mysterious airstrip has been identified as the "Cheshire Airstrip", named after Lewis Carroll's cat that disappears.

Numerous people have claimed that they have knowledge about conspiracy theories surrounding Area 51. Bob Lazar stated that he was contracted by the government in 1989 to work with alien craft that the government had. Bruce Burgess produced a 1996 documentary called Dreamland. The documentary included an interview with a 71 year old man who was a mechanical engineering and said he used the Area 51 facility in the 1950s. The man explained that he had been working to create a flying disc simulator. He also claimed that the simulator was based off a piece of extraterrestrial craft that was found at crash site. This was used for training US pilots. He said that he also had worked with J Rod, an extraterrestrial being who he called a "telepathic savant."

Dan Crain, another man, worked under the pseudonym Dan Burisch. In 2004, he claimed that he had been involved in the cloning virus of alien origin at Area 51.

It has been easy for theories and rumors to surface about Area 51 due to the lack of transparency.

Attack on World Trade Center at 9/11

What happened?

Two planes crashed into New York City's World Trade Center twin buildings on September 11. Another plane crashed into Pentagon, and yet another fell into an open field. 2,996 people were killed and more than 6000 others were injured by the attacks. Although the tragedy was devastating, many people believe that it was not accidental.

What are the theories behind these theories?

There are multiple aspects to the theory that 9/11 was not a tragic accident. This is why the government has covered up the truth. Here is a list of theories surrounding the attack.

1. Stock Traders knew the Attacks Well in Advance of Time

Many investors expressed an interest in buying stocks and stock of American Airlines, right before the plane crashed into the tower. This is because these airlines were the ones that were hijacked to execute the attacks. Many conspiracy theorists believe insurance and stock exchange traders were aware of the attacks in advance and profited. It is not only the horror of using tragedy to make profits, but it is also suspect because they would need to get their information form somewhere. Why wasn't the attack stopped if someone knew?

2. Stand Down Orders by NORAD

Another conspiracy theory is the North American Aerospace Defense Command's (NORAD), which was believed to have the ability to intercept the planes, knew what was happening and did nothing. NORAD may have scrambled fighters too late to allow the planes to reach the Pentagon and tower, instead of intervening and taking them down.

3. Collapse?

The most widely accepted theory about 9/11 is the belief that the impact on the World Trade Center from the planes colliding with it would not have caused it's collapse. In fact, the collapse was caused by strategically placed explosives within the building. This is known as the "demolition Theory." Richard

Gage, Steven E. Jones and Jim Hoffman are some of its supporters. These people assert that fire and impact alone would have not been sufficient to bring down these towers. Furthermore, they wouldn't have fallen as quickly without the help of other factors.

Niels Harrit, Jeffrey Farrer, Steven E. Jones authored an article entitled "Active thermomic material discovered in dust after the 9/11 World Trade Center Catastrophe" in the Open Chemical Physics Journal. It stated that nano-thermite and thermite composites had been found in the debris around the collapsed buildings. This was evidence that explosives were involved and not simply fires.

This theory is believed to be based on the fact that the angles of the collapse and heat contained in the melted metal beams are evidence that buildings did not collapse under the impact.

4. No Plane Hits the Pentagon

Dylan Avery, a filmmaker; and Thierry Messan, a politician, back this theory. They claim American Airlines Flight 77 caused the Pentagon's damage and destruction. They claim that the plane didn't even hit the Pentagon. Instead, they believe it was a missile that crashed into the Pentagon. This missile was launched inside the US, and had ties to the US government. Their theory includes the fact that the Pentagon wall holes were too small for a Boeing757 plane to have made. The hole was 60 feet wide, while a Boeing 757 measures only 155 ft and 125 ft.

5. Fake Phone Calls

Another claim being made by those who claimed the attacks were faked, is that the phone conversations made from the hijacked planes during the doomed flights were faked. The reason this happened is that cell phones couldn't get reception at the same altitude as planes. Another reason the calls seem to be fake or questionable is the fact that one of them, a son calling his mother, used his first-

and last names to refer to himself. This seems unusual and suspicious.

There are many theories around the possible faking terrorist attacks that occurred on 9/11. These are just a few.

JFK Assassination

What has really happened?

On November 22, 1963 President John F. Kennedy rode in an open top limo as he traveled through Dealey Plaza in Dallas. One bullet hit his head, the other his neck. Lee Harvey Oswald was charged as the victim in his murder. Earl Warren who is Chief Justice of the United States Supreme Court stated that Oswald committed the crime alone.

Why is it so odd?

This is the story told in history books. But conspiracy theorists believe something darker. The conspiracy theories surrounding the cover up involve the Mafia. Fidel Cuba, Vice President Lyndon B Johnson and the CIA. People believe Oswald did indeed shoot the president but that he was not the only gunman to do so.

There are many parts to the conspiracy plan to assassinate JFK.

These theories have one thing in common: Oswald wasn't acting alone. Within hours of the shooting, he was arrested and had been arraigned. Oswald died on Sunday after being shot by Jack Ruby while he was being transferred from city jail to county jail. People started to wonder if the president's assassination was part in a bigger plot.

Another element is the number fired shots. The FBI determined that three shots were fired. Two hitting President Kennedy, one hitting Governor Connally and one hitting him and injuring him. Connally was in the limousine with the president. There is speculation that a fourth shot was fired from the nearby grassy slope, and that this was responsible for Kennedy's untimely death. Analysis of what is called the Zapruder Film, an 8mm silent film that runs for 26.6 secs, supports this theory. It depicts the complete assassination. But others believe that there may have been a break in filming. Eyewitnesses claimed there were more than three bullets fired. One reporter even said that she was actually in line of fire.

Another aspect of Kennedy's shooting is under attack is its trajectory. This is in reference to the "singleshot theory", which states that Kennedy was mortally wounded by one bullet. Doctors and nurses at Kennedy’s hospital said that Kennedy's head was hit from the rear, while the back was blown out. Critics say that the bullet should have been able to reverse its course once it went through Kennedy's neck. Critics also suggest that the bullet traveled in a downward direction, which implies that it was shot from the six-floor window of the Book Depository nearby.

A variety of theories are available about the "why." Some believe the president was murdered on the orders of Lyndon B. Johnson his vice president or by CIA agents angered at the Bay of Pigs. Some believe he assassinated him by KGB agents, while others believe it to have been Kennedy's brother because he helped to prosecute organized criminal groups.

Some people believe Oswald was actually a CIA agents or that he had a type of relationship to the Agency and carried their wishes out in assassinating Kennedy. An investigator with the House Select Committee on Assassinations stated that Oswald was being pressured by his colleagues to stop investigating the possible connections between Oswald (CIA) and Kennedy. He claimed that Oswald's assassination was caused by a CIA agent contacting him. The agent also had connections with a Cuban anti Castro group.

The mystery surrounding John F. Kennedy's assassination is one the most persistent and widespread conspiracy theories in America. There are many theories, reasons, and ideas surrounding it. This warrants a closer inspection.

CIA & AIDs

While most people are familiar with AIDs, they may not be aware that it is a naturally occurring virus. However, it has been suggested that it was created by man and was spread by the CIA. It is widely believed that HIV/AIDS first appeared in Africa. It was a virus that originated from monkeys and chimpanzees and then spread to humans. A few people believe that HIV/AIDS actually originated in Manhattan, New York, in 1979. This was several years before it was detected in Africa.

Some believe the virus was introduced by the CIA via inoculations against hepatitis B. These inoculations were based on blood donations from people in the US, most of them gay males. The study was meant to help prevent the spread of hepatitis B to at-risk individuals. It was carried out by the gay community.

The vaccine was developed using both the blood of members of the gay population and the blood of a monkey or chimpanzee. Doctors and scientists soon discovered that many people who had been part of the study were HIV-positive. Some believe that the CIA purposely created the virus in order to rid the gay population of their moral majority and to bring back the moral majority. Others think they were simply using them as scapegoats to create the sinister disease.

Some people believe that HIV was created to thin the population. A pamphlet by an East German Biologist was published in 1986. This was during the first year of the AIDs epidemic. It claimed that scientists at Fort Detrick military laboratory in Maryland created the disease by mixing a Visna, a sheep virus, with a retrovirus causing leukemia, HTLV-1.

There are others who believe that AIDs was created in order to kill the American black population. They believe that HIV was created secretly in New York by scientists at Cold Spring Harbor.

While many believe that the virus has been deliberately created to harm, others argue that it was created accidentally by man. British journalist Hilary Koprowski argued in 1999 that the outbreak was caused by an unintentional human being at the Wistar Research Institute. The doctor used kidneys taken directly from chimps to produce an oral polio vaccine. He claims that the chimps became infected infected in the simian precursor AIDS, SIV. When a mass-vaccination experiment was done in the Belgian Congo, it spread to other species.

There are many conspiracy theories, but one that says AIDs isn't a virus. Some believe that malnutrition causes the disease in Africa while others believe that it is caused by promiscuity or drugs in America. Some believe AIDs is a Biblical pest, sent by God in punishment for the homosexual community in America and the rest of America. They believe that AIDs was specifically a gay plague and their punishments.

AIDs is a terrible disease that caused a great deal of suffering and has continued to be a problem for humanity today. However, not in the extent that it decimated entire communities during the epidemic. It's understandable people would search for answers to the horror. They would try to put the blame on a single person or organisation.

TWA Flight 800, Crash or Missile Attack

What happened?

Trans World Airlines Flight 800 took to the skies from JFK Airport just before sunset on July 17, 1996. It was headed for Paris, France. The Boeing 747131 jetliner flew 230 passengers on that day. The plane was only

11 minutes into the tragic flight and was already flying at 13,700ft above the sea level. This is lower than most planes fly at that altitude. TWA 800 had delayed reaching altitude to allow another plane to descend. TWA 800 was already south of Long Island in New York about 11 minutes into flight. It had just crossed the Atlantic ocean.

TWA 800 lost control of its climb and was unable to reach their cruising altitude. The plane seemed like it was about to explode without warning. Kerosene from the tanks in the middle and wings was dumped, and it vaporized into the air before being ignited. Long Islanders saw the fireball and parts of the plane fell into the water.

Why was that so?

There were several eyewitnesses present at the scene of the crash who were interviewed for radio and television. They said they had seen an unusual sight right before it exploded. They stated that there was something in the sky that flew toward the plane. The object was bright and turned midair once it got close. They also claimed it moved vertically and horizontally. The fact that so many people saw it clearly from different directions meant that it must have been very close to the plane. This was not an optical illusion. Eyewitnesses were not the only ones who claimed to have seen strange objects in the skies. Other pilots were also flying at the same time and claimed to have seen something right near the plane. The plane appears to have been taken down.

FBI interviewed 154 witnesses. All of them said that they had witnessed a missile moving through the sky towards the plane, just before it exploded. These were military personnel, scientists, academics, and business leaders.

The government seemed to want to discourage people from looking too closely. This may indicate a coverup. The Navy and FBI released information that appeared to indicate that TWA 800 harbored something dangerous, possibly something biological, which could make it extremely dangerous for any individual who was to come in contact. People reported seeing soldiers dressed in bio-suits strolling along Long Island beaches next to the crash site.

Officials claimed there was no explosive residue, but it was later discovered that this was false information. It was also believed that the public was hiding the truth. Many believed that it was a simple test missile failure. However, the truth was finally revealed. They found explosive residue in the debris.

According to the government's official story, the plane crashed because the fuel vapors inside the fuel tank at their center burst suddenly. The plane continued climbing until it crashed. People mistakenly believed that the plane was being shot at from the sky. They claim the plane then crashed and exploded into the water. Skeptics refute this story.

The official story doesn't align with what about 200 eyewitnesses claim they saw. It would mean that each person who claimed to see something different than that story was mistaken. That they mistook a single plane in the air as a missile heading towards a aircraft.

Skeptics also question the official story. They say that a 747 lacking a nose couldn't remain in a stable flight long to climb as claimed by the government. However, calculations and model simulations have shown that this theory is false.

People are also skeptical of this story because of the Navy's strange involvement in the proceedings. The Navy sent its most powerful deep-sea salvage ships to the crash site immediately after it happened. They took control of salvage and kicked out New York Police Department divers who had been there before them. The Navy was able to search the bottom of half of Rhode Island's ocean floor while soldiers cleaned the beaches. The Navy justified its extensive involvement by claiming that they couldn’t find the flight records, also known to as “black boxes”, even though many private boat owner were claiming that their sonar was picking up locator pulses from the boxes. The Navy eventually admitted that there were at least three subs in the vicinity at the time of the plane's crash.

Although the government claimed that the plane had just exploded out-of-control, many believe it was actually shot out of the heavens.

UFO Landings, Aliens and UFOs in America

There have been reports all over the country about strange lights, strange vehicles flying through airspace, and strange crashes. These reports have been filed for years and ignored by the US government. There are many who believe that America has had contact with extraterrestrial intelligence and that there have also been many landings and crashes of aircraft on the soil.

Roswell, New Mexico, is perhaps the most well known example. Many experts believe that the "Roswell Incident", also known as the United States Government's coverup of contact with extraterrestrials, is one the most glaring evidence that the United States has lied about.

The event itself occurred approximately 75 miles from Roswell. After a ranch worker reported it, debris was found at a ranch. A press release that day claimed that a "flying device" had crashed on the ranch during severe weather conditions. Later, the story seemed different. Now, the media was claiming that it was weather balloon, and reporters were shown debris which included rubber, wood, and foil.

Official records state that the debris discovered at the ranch was an experiment in technology called Project Mogul. Project Mogul was supposed detect sound waves found in the upper levels, which were caused by Soviet nuclear bombs. Many people are skeptical about this story. Many books discrediting the story appeared over the years, claiming it was an alien craft that crashed on the ranch. The weather balloon story was also a coverup. Some claimed that a gouge was made of the area near the crash site. Some claimed that witnesses saw a highly secretive, extensive recovery operation at the ranch. However, they were turned down by armed soldiers. One book said that there was an archeology group present that saw the alien debris and bodies. People believe that the alien spacecraft crashed on Roswell Ranch. According to one book, the government recovered the alien bodies and took them to a secure location for autopsies.

UFO landings were also reported in other parts of the US. Gordon Cooper (an astronaut) claims that he witnessed an UFO landing at Edwards Air Force Base. According to his story, he was a member of an elite group of test pilots at Edwards Air Force Base that was in charge for several advanced projects. A camera crew was filming a precision landing system installation when he witnessed a flying saucer. They were filming the flight of the saucer overhead. Then they saw it hover above them, extend three legs for landing gear, and then come to rest on dry lakebed. He said that the cameramen had been able to film within 30 meters of the crash site. He claimed that the "classic saucer" was smooth and shiny. He said that the UFO was approximately 30 feet across. He claimed that it flew again after they got close to the UFO. Cooper was then ordered to develop the film, and then give it to Washington. This was denied by the government.

Those who think that the government is concealing contact with extraterrestrials believe that they do so in order to continue to cover the lies they started telling after World War II. Cooper says they didn't want the public to be aware of UFOs at that time. It was done to keep people from panicking. Cooper claims they kept UFOs under wraps throughout the Cold War.

Many Americans believe that intelligent life has visited the United States many times. Some believe these visitors are angels sent to protect mankind. Some believe they are responsible for all of life on Earth. Some believe aliens are Gods. They create life on Earth and return to guard it. Some people believe that intelligent life has come to play with us, to take us out into all of the universe.

Apollo Moon Landing: Faked?

Apollo 11 was launched to the Moon on July 20, 1969. Buzz Aldrin was the first man to step foot on a moon surface. They did not actually make it to the moon. Many people believe that the initial moon landing and all subsequent landings were faked. There are many factors that could be considered to discredit the landings.

Some people doubt that we actually landed on moon. They claim the main reason why the government faked it was that they were trying to beat the Russians at the space race. But in 1969 we were not even close to being able support humankind and launch a spacecraft to reach the moon. We would be seen as having advanced technology, and the money necessary to fund such an undertaking, if we could land on moon. The Cold War was quietly raging so the US wanted evidence that it was strong enough and secure to take on the risk of sending people there. Doubters suggest that the government faked an actual moon landing because our technology wasn't there.

Others argue that NASA falsified the first and subsequent moon landings to ensure that it received funding. Many theorists believe it was impossible to send men from Earth to the moon in 1969. They claim that NASA raised $30 billion for the project. However, this money could have been used for paying people who owed them. Doubters contend that NASA also faked landings to accomplish President Kennedy's goal. He stated in 1961 that NASA would be landing a man to the moon and bringing him back safely to Earth within the decade. NASA had to do something because time was running out. Skeptics think that something was faking a landing.

People believe that there was another reason to fake the landing. It was done to distract people's attention from the Vietnam War, which is very unpopular. People were so focused upon the space race and so excited to see someone walking on the surface the moon that the government was still able carry out its war efforts without too much backlash. This theory has been supported by those who believe it because the manned land efforts seem to have ended as soon as the US left the war.

Many evidences that skeptics believe are proof that the landings were fraudulently documented. This list will contain only a few, but more information can be found about the theories.

Many people examine the photographs and films made while they were supposed to be on the moon. Some are critical of the images. Others point out flaws. While others believe that the moon's extreme temperature wouldn't have allowed for filming or photographs, some say that the film would have melted if it had. Skeptics think that since there aren't stars in the photos it is likely that astronauts were not in orbit. This especially considering that the astronauts claimed in a press release after the mission, that they had never seen any stars with their naked eye. Skeptics contend that the shadows and angles in the photographs and film are strange. Skeptics use the famous images of a flag of America that was placed on the lunar surface during the first landing. The supporters of the theory that the landing wasn't real claim that the flag appears as if it is waving in wind.

Another reason that landings are alleged to have been faked is environmental factors. Skeptics think that astronauts cannot have survived the trip up to the moon as it would require traveling beyond the Van Allen boundaries. Proponents say that radiation from the Van Allen Belts is trapped in magnetic fields. They also believe that there would have been health dangers if the radiation reached the belts. These experts also believe that this radiation level would have caused fogging to the camera film. It is also claimed that the footprints left on the moon by people were impossible due to the fact that moisture is needed for such a thing. People say the footprint was impossible because of the lack of water on the Moon.

There are many reasons why people believe the moon has never been landed. And they have many examples to back it up. It is an intriguing topic, which merits further study.

Reptilian Rulers

You might believe you know who's in charge. You might be familiar in some countries with the president, vice-president, and kings/queens. Some people believe that they have the ultimate power of shaping our lives. Many people believe that this is false. Many believe that there is a race or reptilian species that control the planet. They have also infiltrated our society so that they are difficult to recognize.

There are two types of origin stories that are widely believed. One theory states that reptilians developed on Earth with other life forms. The theory goes that they master intergalactic transport and left Earth, only for them to return millions upon millions of centuries later to control us all and influence our development. Another theory is that they are originally from Draco and came here thousands years ago, sharing this planet with us. They eventually went into hiding, either through force or choice.

They also claim that they interbred human beings with theirs, and that this has altered our DNA. They say this was done to limit our brain capacity so they could control us. They claim that they also altered our DNA in order to be able to possess us. In the lower fourth dimension, those who were possessed and ruled over by reptilians were called demigods. They say these hybrids gained power over ancient civilizations like Babylonia, Sumer,

Mesopotamia, and Babylon. Then, they insinuated them into the royal family around the globe as humanity grew.

The theory is that reptilians rule every country on the planet and have set up a prison in every corner of the globe to confine and control people, even though they don't know it. They claim that they achieved this by creating borders and controlling the media. This gave them something to fight over. Another theory that supports this theory is that reptilians are poisoning water, food and air in order to make humanity more lazy and dumber and easier to control.

According to this theory, as well as many others who believe in it, there are two types or reptilians that work in our society. Those who are pureblooded and believe they are reptilians. These people can transform their appearance into human-like creatures. Then there are those who believe they are human but actually are a crossbreed between reptilian humans and reptilians. They can be controlled to promote the New World Order.

It is believed that the appearance of humans can help you tell if they are reptilians or not. They are usually described as white people with hazel eyes and green or blue eyes. Unexplained scarring, lower blood pressure and other unusual characteristics are common. It is believed that reptilians lack empathy and are incapable of expressing love the way humans do. They are also believed to be highly intelligent and to love space and science. People claim that you can view the reptilians' true forms by slow motion TV. This allows you to see distortions, such as greenness, scaliness, or skin color.

Many people are believed be reptilian. These include families such the Rockefellers (and the Rothschilds) and the House of Windsor (in Britain). Many of the presidents believed to be reptilians include Barack Obama, Bush Jr., Bill, and Hillary Clinton. These people also believe that many entertainers may be lizards, like Bob Hope (and Brad Pitt).

Reptilians eat both blood and brains, according to some theories. Some theorists believe that reptiles prefer children to adults, since they aren't as poisonous.

Believers of this theory point to the Bible as evidence. There are passages in Bible that mention humans interbreeding alongside Nephilim. While it is unclear if the meaning of the word "Those who Have Descended" is correct, theorists think that the reptilians may be from another planet, or they have returned. Therefore, they are thought to have descended directly from the heavens. They believe that Nephilim were not angels (as many Christians believe), but reptilians who bred alongside humans. The passage also states that the offspring were considered heroes and men to be admired, which is believed to prove that reptilians continued to be influential in their time.

Holocaust Denial

Adolf Hitler commanded the systematic assimilation of six million Jewish people between 1941-45. This genocide is considered to be one of the most deadly in history. It was part a wider set of Nazi party's actions to oppress, kill and destroy different ethnic and political groups throughout Europe. About 200,000 people are responsible for the acts that took these people's lives. Adolf Hitler orchestrated the Holocaust in an effort to eradicate the Jewish race that he saw as inferior. He actually considered many groups inferior and sought their elimination. I was horrified, and survivors of death camps that survived are still able to recall the pain and suffering experienced there.

There is an astonishing number of people who believe that the Holocaust did not occur. These people have many reasons for believing so, as well as things that they consider proof.

Holocaust deniers maintain that the myth exists for one reason: the Jews created it to their benefit, to cash in on it and profit from the restitution Germany would pay. They also believe that the Allies created this myth to justify occupying Germany during World War II. They allege that there is a conspiracy among the Allied powers and Israel to use Holocaust for their own ends, as well as to justify establishing State of Israel.

Holocaust deniers find it easy to ignore what many consider incontrovertible evidence it occurred, and instead claim that it was all a hoax. They claim that the Allied nations tortured those who had taken part in the Holocaust to get confessions. They claim that very few Jewish people actually died during this period, either from natural causes (or were executed for crimes).

One reason that deniers claim the Holocaust didn't occur is that the gas chambers wouldn't have worked the way they were made. They argue that because the chambers had not been hermetically sealed, gas would have leaked out, poisoning those who tried to do the gassing. They also said that it was impossible to verify that the number died of Jews is correct. Also, historians and authorities have not reported that they have found mass graves or piles of bodies. They state that the Allies made it clear that Jewish prisoners who died in concentration camps due to lack of food supply were actually starving. This was not done by the Germans. They claim that survivors have fake tattoos. The Germans would never have attempted to tattoo prisoners they wanted to slaughter. They claim that there were not enough ovens to create large numbers of bodies and that they were only used to make sure that those who died from contagious illnesses while in POW camps were buried. They claim the photos were faked, and that they are propaganda.

The disappearance of so many Jewish people can be explained by claiming that they immigrated to the United States. They just left Germany in order to set up lucrative businesses and shops in the United States.

While it seems unlikely that the Holocaust never took place, there are many who still believe in it and defend them vigorously.

The holocaust in which the Jews were murdered was not the first or last extermination to be called into question. It is possible for a group to go through denial about atrocities because it is inconceivable and not able to be defended. So it was with the Turkish genocide that took place in Turkey against the Armenians during World War I (1914-1918). New York Time and other newspapers have numerous reports that show how Turks killed men and boys, then marched women and children into deserts to die or sell them to local tribes. Despite numerous survivors telling their stories, the Turkish government still refuses to admit that they were involved in the massacre of over 1,000,000 Armenians. People can do terrible acts, but then they must lie about it. Amazingly, not only does the Turkish government deny any involvement but they also say that it simply didn't happen. It is also about the cash. If the Turkish government was to admit they were involved they could be forced to pay reparations to Armenians and return any property they owned at the time.

Shakespeare Was There?

To be, or not to become? William Shakespeare is, evidently, the subject of this question. He is undoubtedly the most well-known playwright today, but some people believe that he does not exist, or that he did no author any of the works which are attributed to him.

Doubt over Shakespeare's identity emerged in the late 19th and has since become mainstream. The Globe Theater in London was founded by the former artistic chief of Shakespeare's Globe Theater. It is a modern, replica of Shakespeare's own theater that plays plays. In a "Declaration of Reasonable Doubt", the two authors stated that there are still questions about Shakespeare's identity. Participants in this work or those who approved its validity include the former LA Times arts editor, an English professor in Washington State, as well as a Rutgers social science professor.

Theorists believe many pieces are evidence to back their arguments. However, it is difficult to discuss because William Shakespeare was bad at leaving evidence from his life. It is difficult to determine if he signed any of his work. The signatures he did sign on works are so sloppy and indecipherable that it is hard for anyone to believe they were his. They haven't been able to locate any Shakespeare-authorized letters, poems, or plays. And his will does not mention books, plays, or any other evidence that William Shakespeare, a balding Stratford businessman, was a author.

Biographically, not much is known about William Shakespeare. The main facts are that he was a market boy who was born, raised and buried in Stratford-Upon-Avon. It is about 100 miles from London. Stratford was a known place for trading wool and tanning, as well as marketing and slaughtering sheep. His father was a glover while his mother belonged to the local gentry. Both of their signatures were not signed by them, but they did sign their names with marks. Furthermore, there is no evidence that Shakespeare was educated. According to those who believe Shakespeare did NOT write his works, their backgrounds were not compatible with the types of people who would have written them. The author of those works is believed to have had knowledge about politics, court culture, and the sports enjoyed by the aristocracy. This includes lawn-bowling falconry, tennis, and falconry. This theory suggests that the son a glover wasn't likely to have these experiences.

Anti-Stratfordians (the majority of theorists) believe that William Shakespeare was a cover or pseudonym used by the author to conceal their true identity. Anti-Stratfordians are not the only ones who claim Shakespeare's writings were written by others. Here are a few examples.

Christopher Marlowe

Christopher Marlowe (also a playwright) was writing around Shakespeare's time. Proponents of this theory claim that Christopher Marlowe died in a brawl near the end of May 1593. However, they also believe that the report was faked to keep Marlowe out of prison for atheism. Marlovits, people who believe this theory, say Shakespeare was cited in Marlowe's works to hide the truth that Marlowe was still alive.

Edward de Vere

This man, Earl of Oxford and Lord Great Courtlain of England, was also an important courtier poet. Many believe Edward de Vere may have been Shakespeare's original author. He was more educated than Shakespeare and had more experience in poetry and court. Shakespeare's work looks like it was written by a skilled courtier who is familiar with the intrigues in a royal court. People who believe Shakespeare didn't write his works state that he simply didn't have the experience required to create works with this feel. They also believe that Shakespeare's works have references to de Vere's times and that de Vere himself is the author.

William Stanley

William Stanley is another important individual and another Earl. This makes him a potential contender for several reasons. Stanley, the sixth Earl and Chief Justice of Derby, was educated and experienced in the courtly life. His theater company was his business, so he also had a background with plays. Another interesting point is that he used to call himself Will. He also signed things with this name, something William Shakespeare was known for.

Nearly everyone agrees the works of William Shakespeare are masterful works. But, some don't believe it was William Shakespeare who wrote them.

Chemtrails

If you've ever been outdoors on a clear and sunny day, then you've probably seen the trails left behind from airplanes. These are often called "contrails," which is a portmanteau term for condensation trails. They have been explained as condensation left behind in air by airplanes.

But there are others who doubt this explanation. These people call these chemical trails chemtrails. They believe they are made up of chemicals. They believe these chemicals are intentionally released into air to serve different purposes depending on who is arguing. Some people believe that these chemicals might be released in order to control population, manipulate people psychologically or modify the weather or manage solar radiation. Many believe that the chemicals are responsible for many health problems including respiratory infections.

The United States Air Force published a 1996 study on weather modification. The report covered weather modification. Afterward, the

Air Force faced accusations of spraying unknown chemicals over the US. The accused posted their theories on forums and the internet. Later, a late-night radio host discussed the theories. The EPA was able to provide a response in 200. But, it is not clear if the conspiracy theory supporters are correct.

So, what exactly are chemtrails and how do they work?

According to this theory, chemtrails could be distinguished from harmless contrails through their appearance and duration. They state that chemtrails could last for half a days in the sky, or can turn into cirrus clouds. Other indicators of chemtrails may include visible colors in the stream, clusters of trails within a small area, or trails left behind by military aircraft or unmarked planes flying high above their normal altitudes.

Chemtrails contain such substances as barium salts, thorium silicon carbide, lithium and polymer fibers.

This theory states that some people have reported seeing unusual activity in their skies. They have reported seeing planes leaving trails at lower altitudes. The trails are parallel, form S's and then X's. Also, they saw trails that were asymmetrical, which is a combination of s's and x's. They have reported unusual tastes and smells as well as getting sick from the chemtrails.

What believe the theorists of conspiracy theory?

Many people who believe in this theory think that chemtrails form part of a larger conspiracy. This conspiracy has many objectives, such as population control, testing weapons or weather-based weapons, making people sick for drug companies to profit. People also claim that the government could be releasing vaccines directly into the atmosphere to inoculate citizens against their will.

Conclusion

Congratulations on your quest to discover some of most controversial theories worldwide.

I hope this book was entertaining.

These theories should not be presented to you in an attempt to confuse you. Instead, they are meant to increase your imagination.

Although the evidence will prove some theories wrong, there will still be new information.

We appreciate your support and wish you every success!

9 781774 856192

www.ingramcontent.com/pod-product-compliance
Lightning Source LLC
Chambersburg PA
CBHW050359120526
44590CB00015B/1748
* 9 7 8 1 7 7 4 8 5 6 1 9 2 *